Sean Kenney

Totally Cool Creations

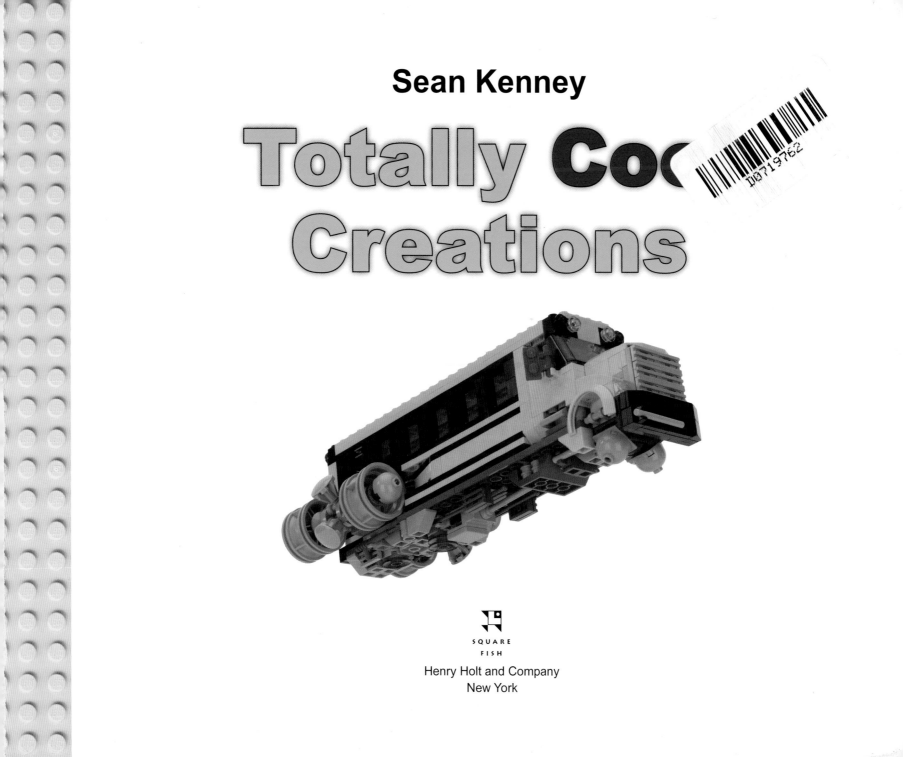

SQUARE
FISH

Henry Holt and Company
New York

SQUARE
FISH

An Imprint of Macmillan
175 Fifth Avenue
New York, NY 10010
mackids.com

Printed in China by South China Printing Company Ltd.,
Dongguan City, Guangdong Province

Square Fish and the Square Fish logo are trademarks of Macmillan and
are used by Christy Ottaviano Books/Henry Holt and Company under license from
Macmillan.

LEGO®, the brick configuration, and the minifigure are trademarks of the LEGO Group,
which does not sponsor, authorize, or endorse the book.

Square Fish books may be purchased for business or promotional use. For information
on bulk purchases, please contact the Macmillan Corporate and Premium Sales
Department at (800) 221-7945 x 5442 or by e-mail at specialmarkets@macmillan.com.

Originally published in the United States by
Christy Ottaviano Books/Henry Holt and Company
First Square Fish Edition: September 2013
Book designed by Elynn Cohen
LEGO bricks were used to create the models for this book.
The models were photographed by John E. Barrett, with the exception of pages 3, 10,
11, 32, 33, 34, 50, 51, 72, 73, 96, 97, 98, 99, 100, 101, 102, 104, 105, 112, and 113,
which were photographed by Sean Kenney.
Square Fish logo designed by Filomena Tuosto

10 9 8 7 6 5 4 3 2 1

Contents

Cool Cars and Trucks  5

Cool Robots 43

Cool City 81

Let's Ask Sean 124

Cool Cars and Trucks

Let's build some cars!

Here come the cool cars!	9
Car carrier	10
SUV	12
Taxis of all sizes	15
Too fast!	16
Load the airplane	18
Strong builders and heavy haulers	20
Pocket-sized crazy cars	24
Rush to the rescue!	26
Wide load	28
Make your own truck	31
Build a wide-load flatbed	32
Moving day	35
Around your neighborhood	36
Tune it up	38
Flatten it down	39
Build it BIG!	40

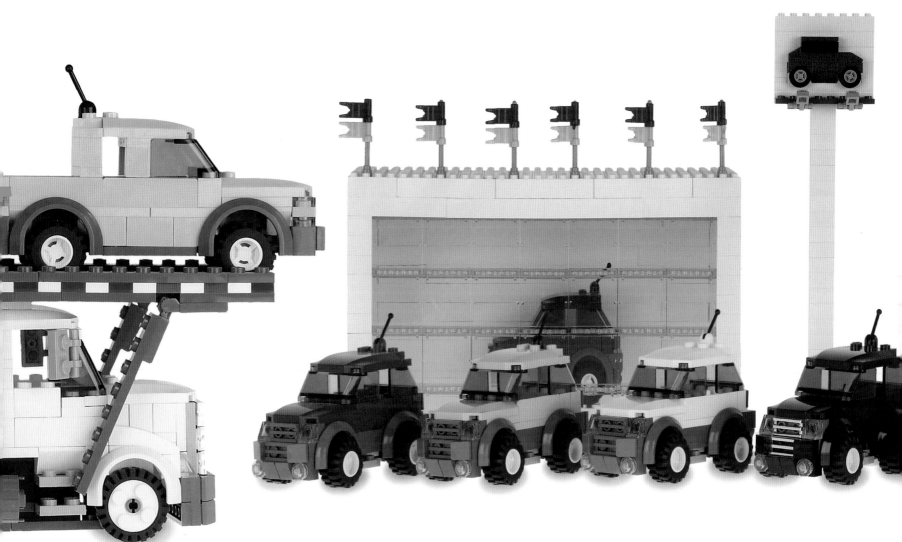

Here come the cool cars!

A big car carrier brings lots of cars and trucks to
the auto dealership.

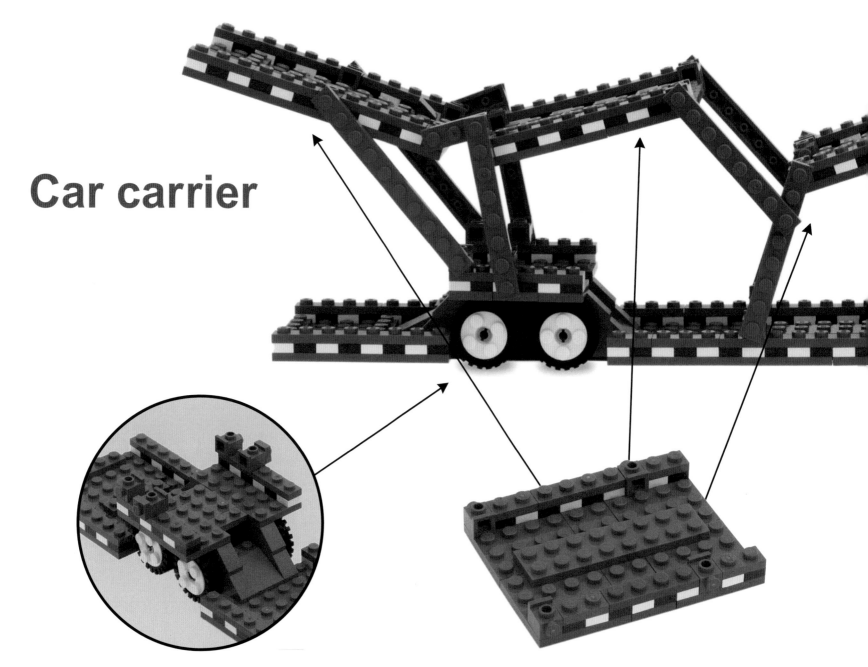

Car carrier

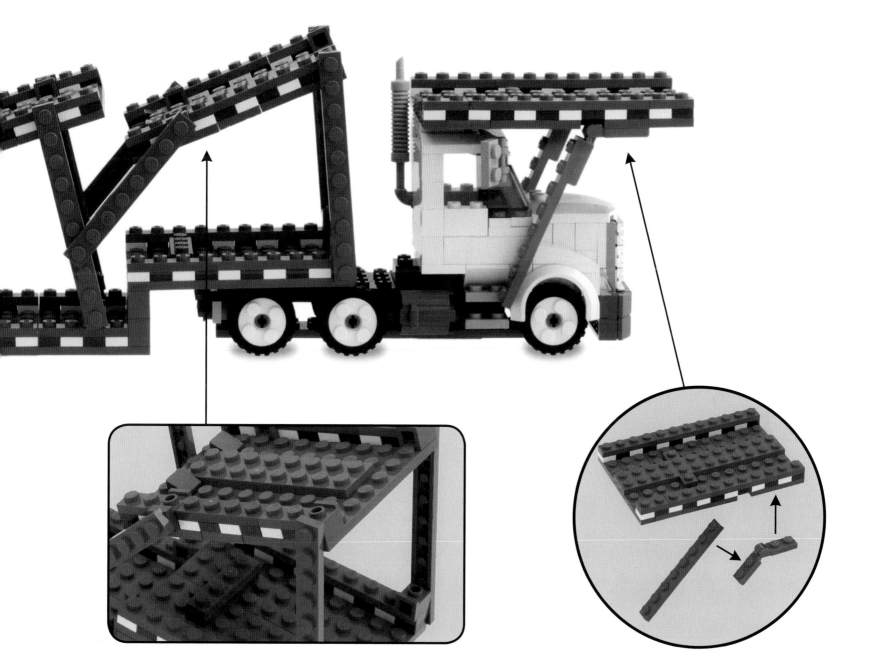

SUV

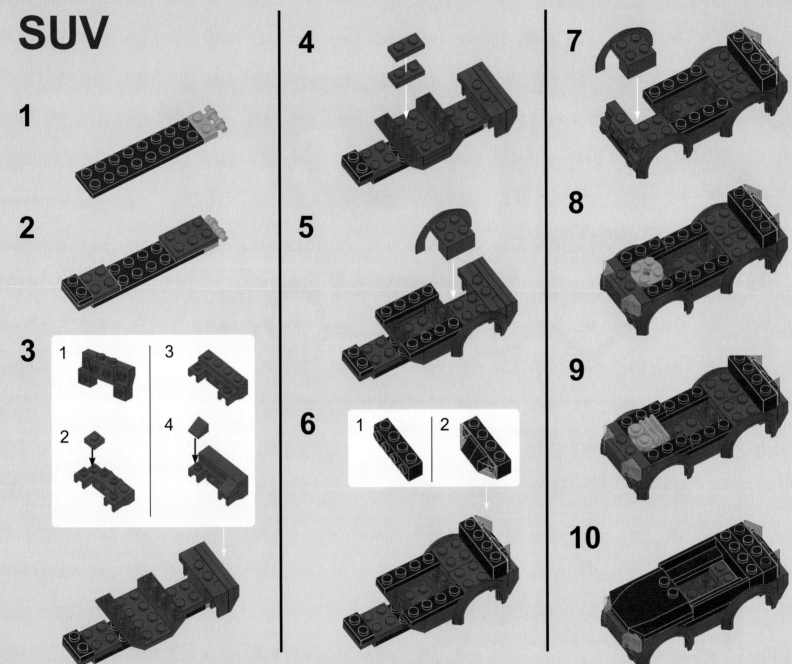

1

2

3
1
2
3
4

4

5

6
1
2

7

8

9

10

11

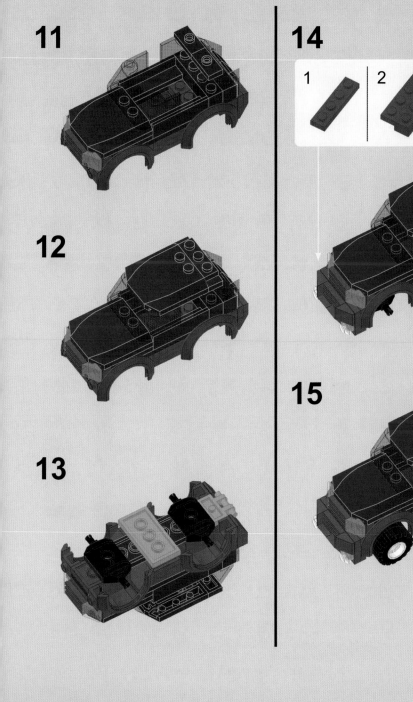

12

13

14

1 2 3

15

Can you change the SUV to look like these cars?

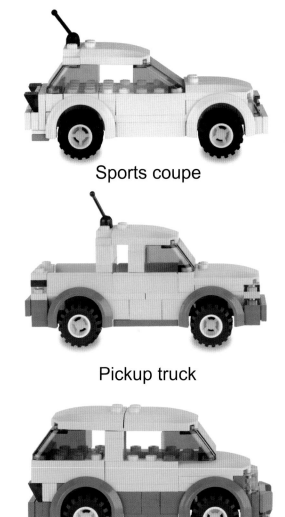

Sports coupe

Pickup truck

Minivan

Taxis of all sizes

If you don't have enough LEGO
pieces to build a big car, try
making the same car
in a smaller size.

Too fast!

Sporty cars can drive fast but speeders better watch out.

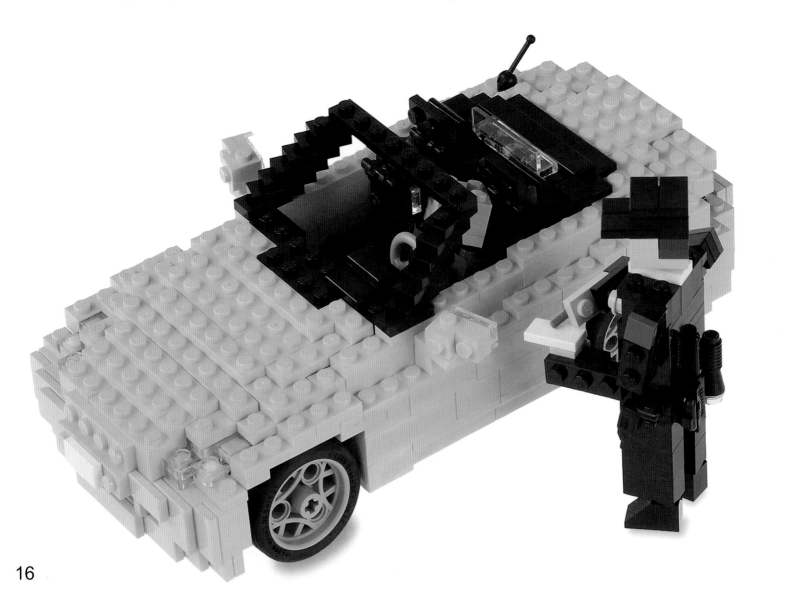

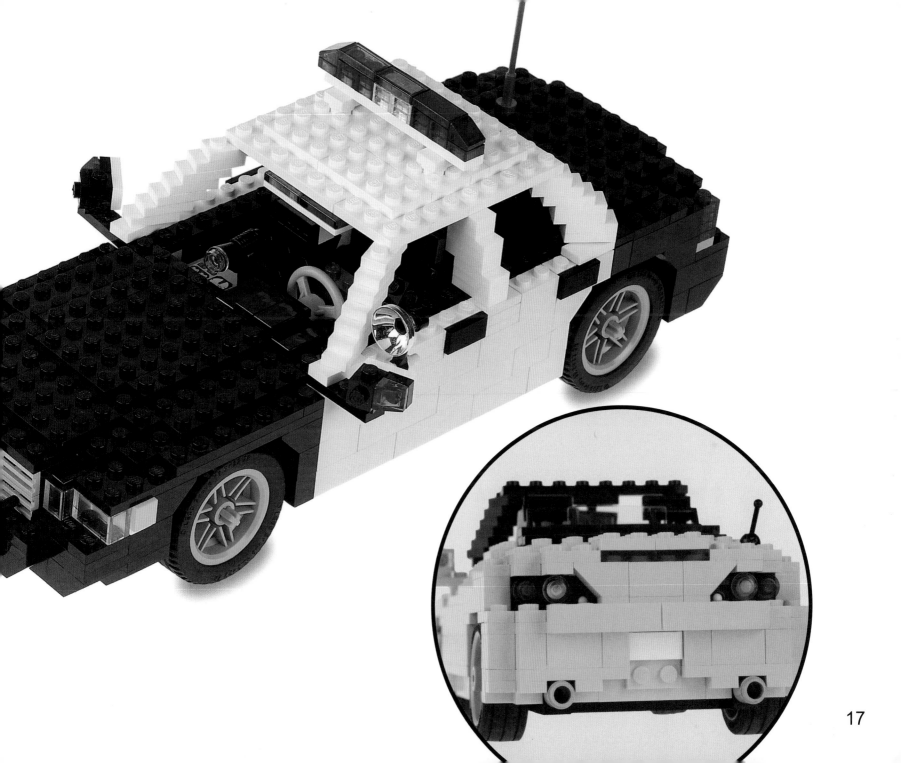

Load the airplane

These tough little airport vehicles have to hurry to get passengers and luggage onto the plane in time for takeoff.

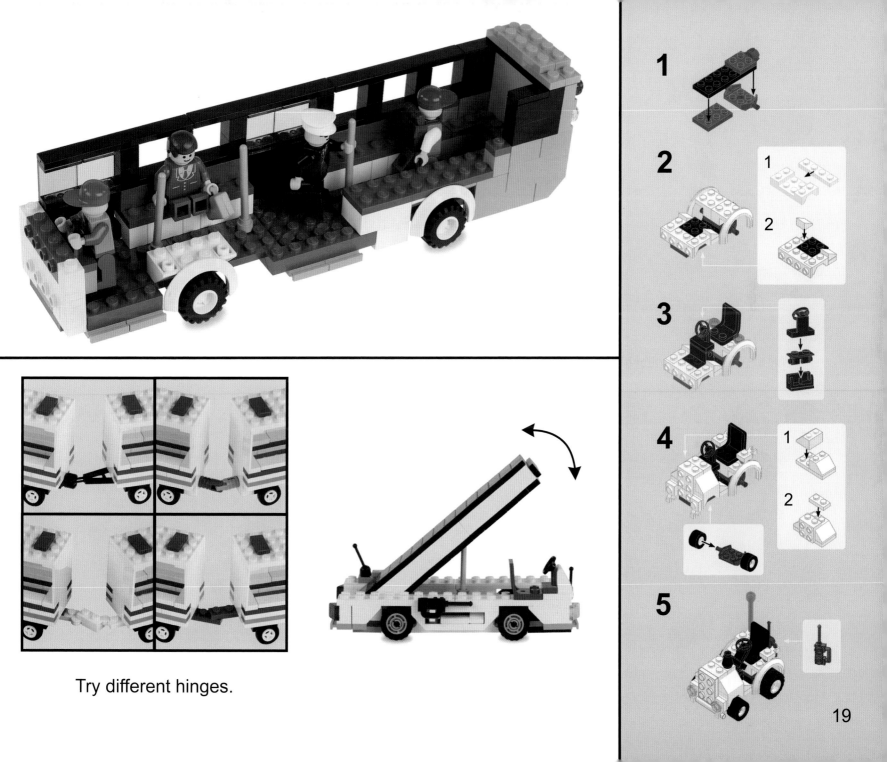

Try different hinges.

1

2

3

4

5

19

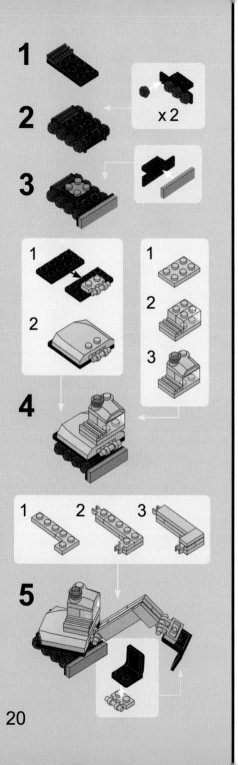

Strong builders and heavy haulers

Strong trucks move lots of dirt, rocks, cement, and steel to help construct buildings.

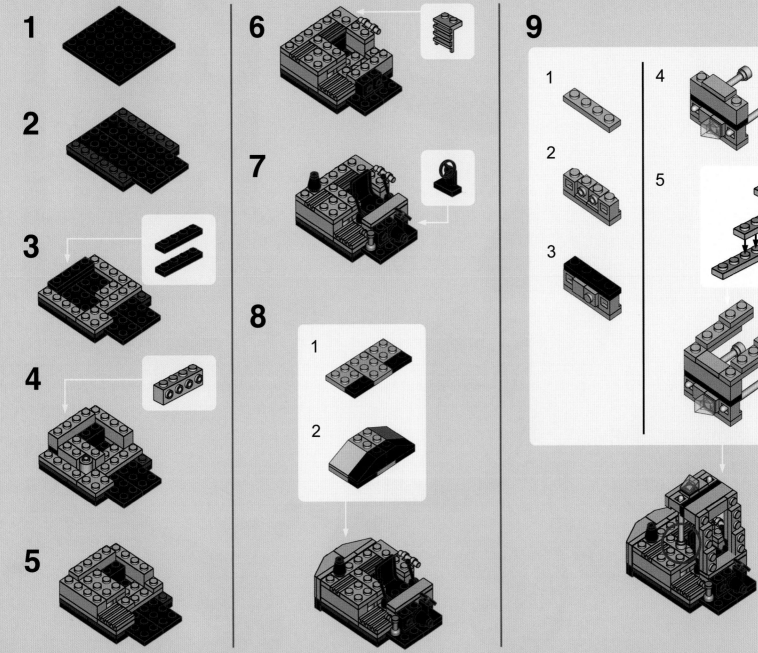

10

1

2

3

4

1

2

5

1

2

3

6

1

2

11

1

2

3

4

5

6

7

1

2

x 2

1

2

Excavator

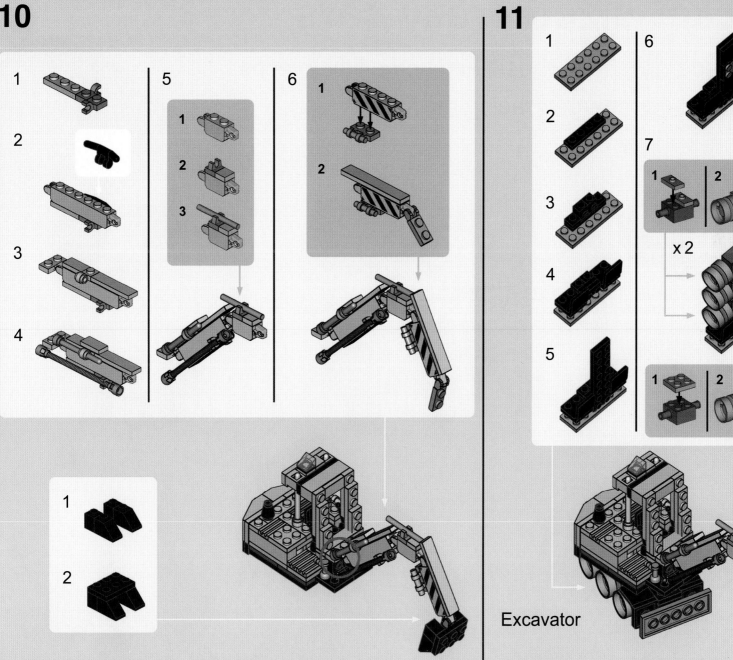

Pocket-sized crazy cars

You need only a few wheels and some little pieces to build a turbocharged racing machine.

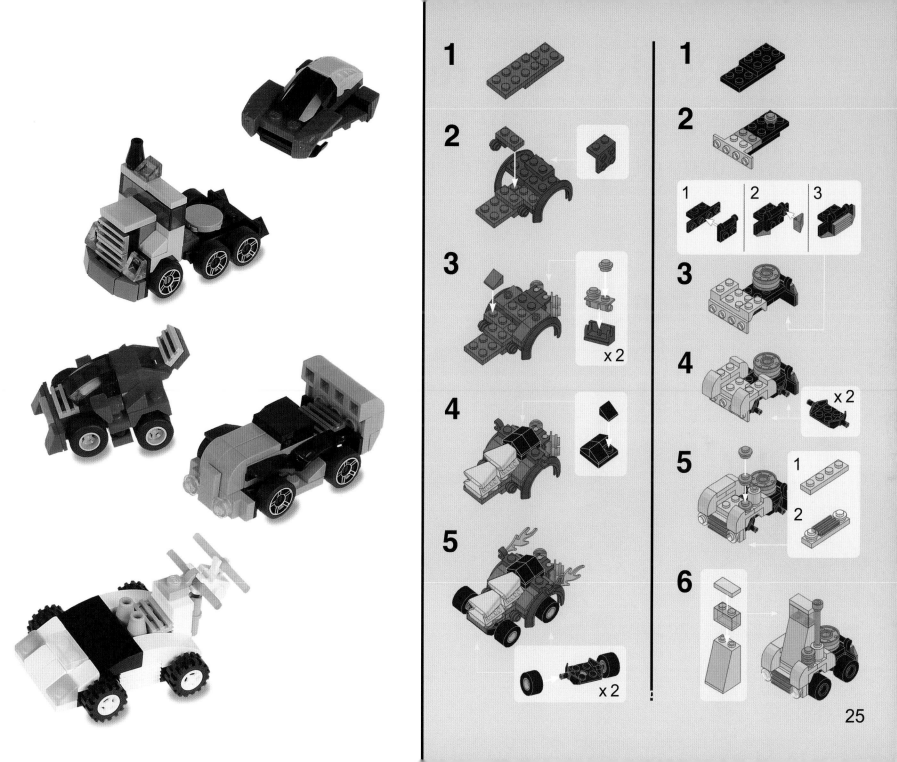

1

2 x2

3 x2

4

5 x2

1

2

1 | 2 | 3

3

4 x2

5 1 2

6

Rush to the rescue!

Fire trucks, police cars, and ambulances hurry off to save people's lives.

Wide load

Sometimes trucks move really big things, like a house!

1

2

3

4

5

6 x2

7

8 x2

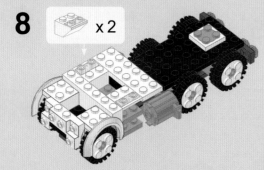

9

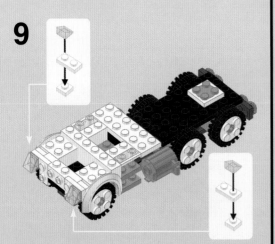

10

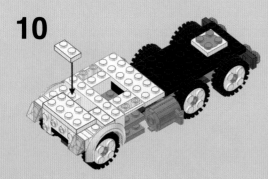

11

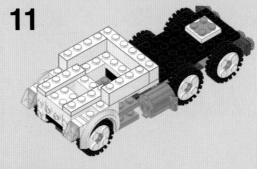

12

| 1 | 2 | 3 |

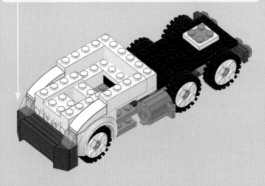

13

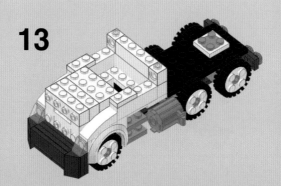

14

15

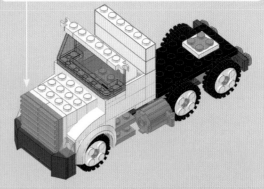

| 1 | 2 | 3 |

16

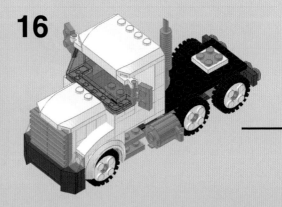

Make your own truck

You can use the same basic design to create many other trucks.

Build a wide-load flatbed

What other kinds of furniture can you make?

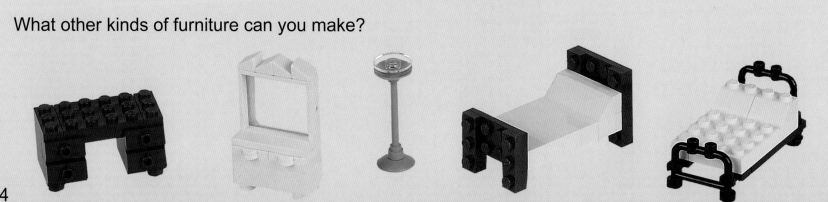

Moving day

A moving truck with a ramp and lots of doors makes it easy to carry furniture and boxes to a new house.

Around your neighborhood

Every day, cool cars are all around, bringing packages, fixing your street, even selling ice cream!

Tune it up

Switch out engines, fenders, wheels, and more to turn a regular car into a street racer.

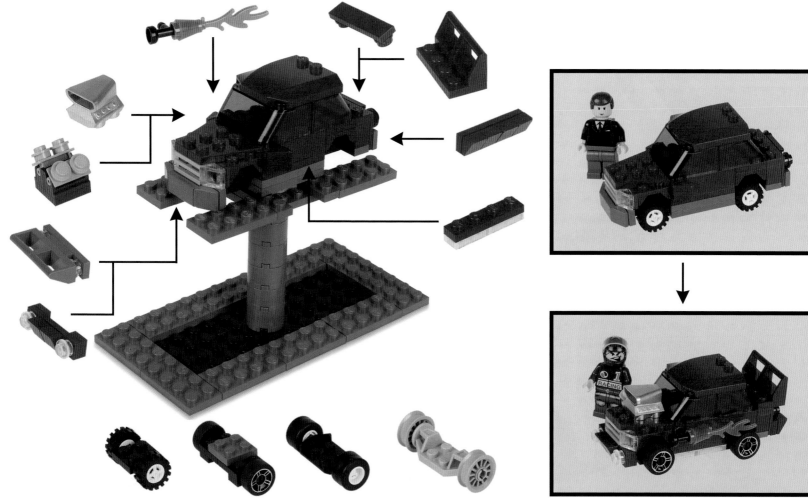

Flatten it down

Build a mosaic by creating a flat picture of a car.

Build it BIG!

Create giant versions of LEGO bricks,
then combine them into a giant car.

These large bricks are 6 times the size of regular bricks.

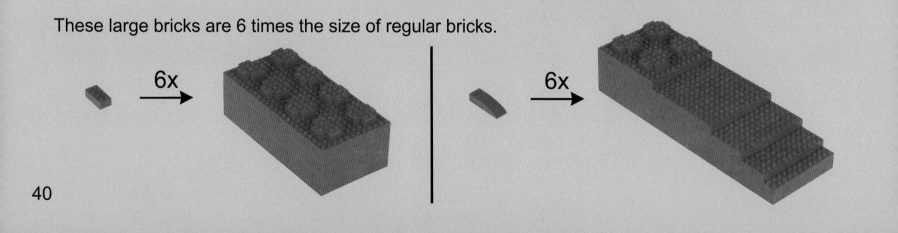

6x

6x

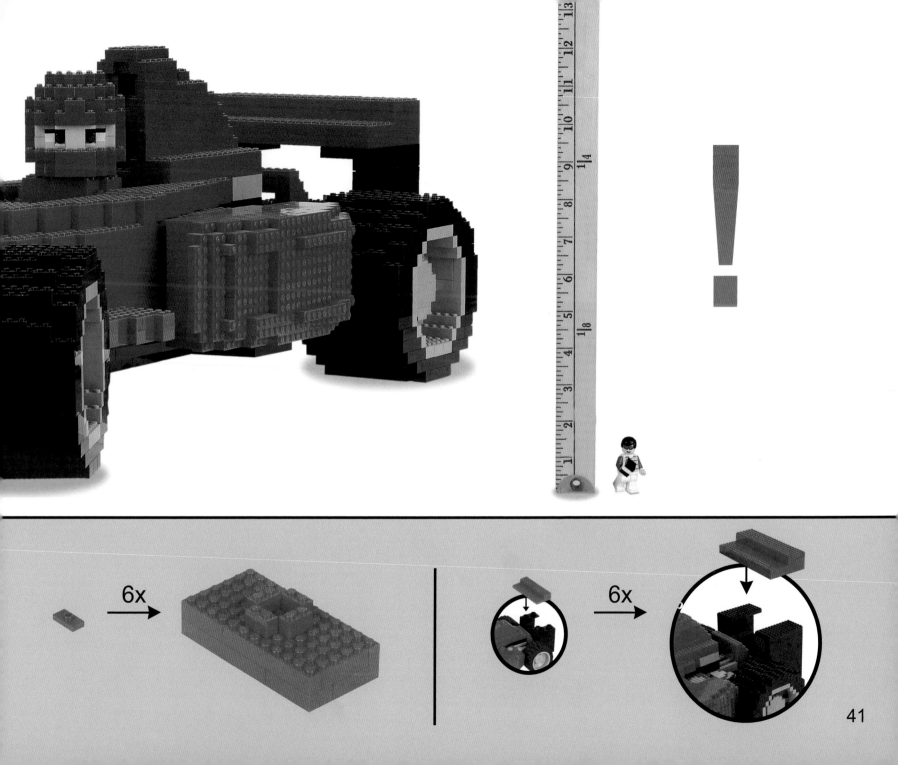

6x

6x

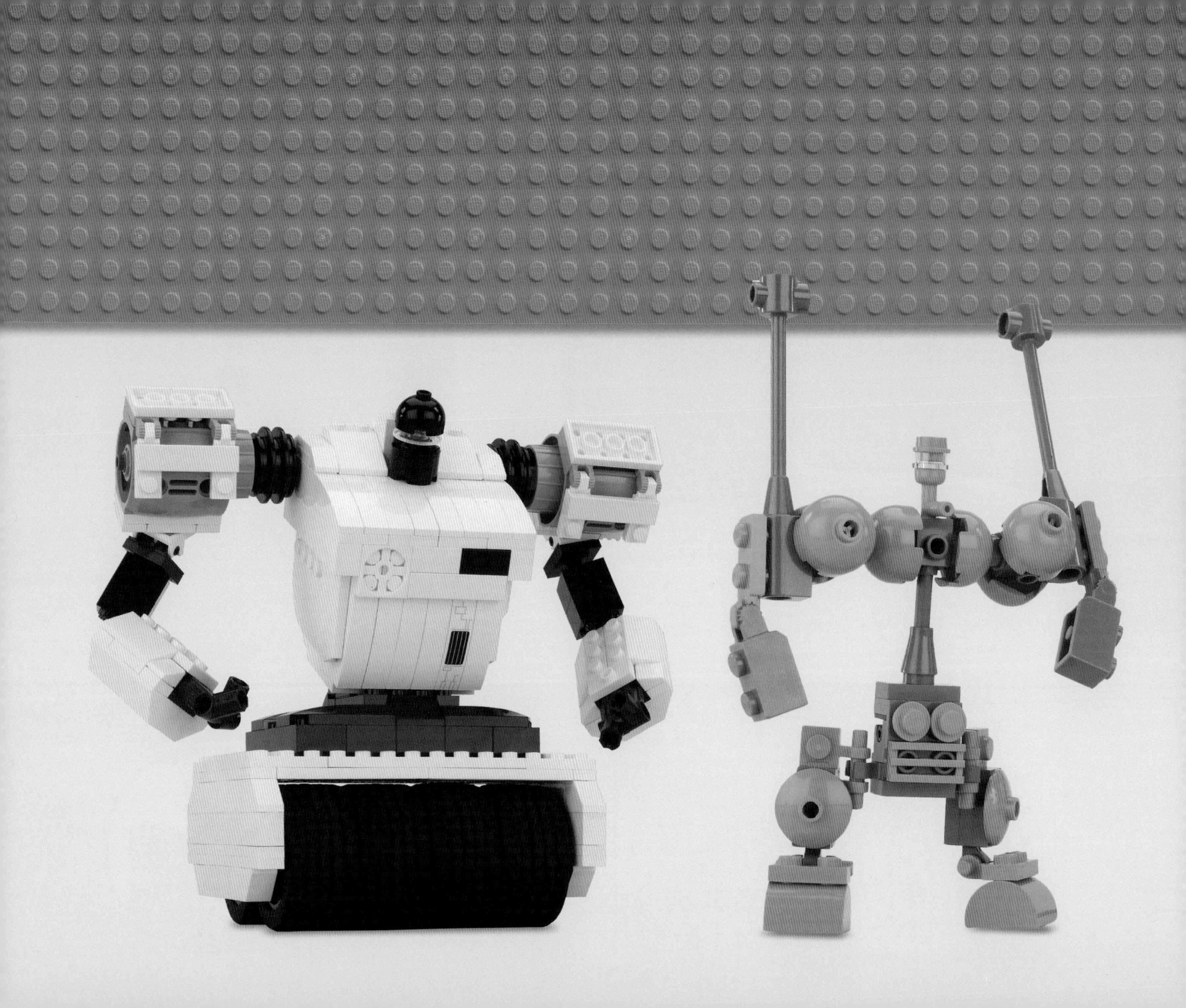

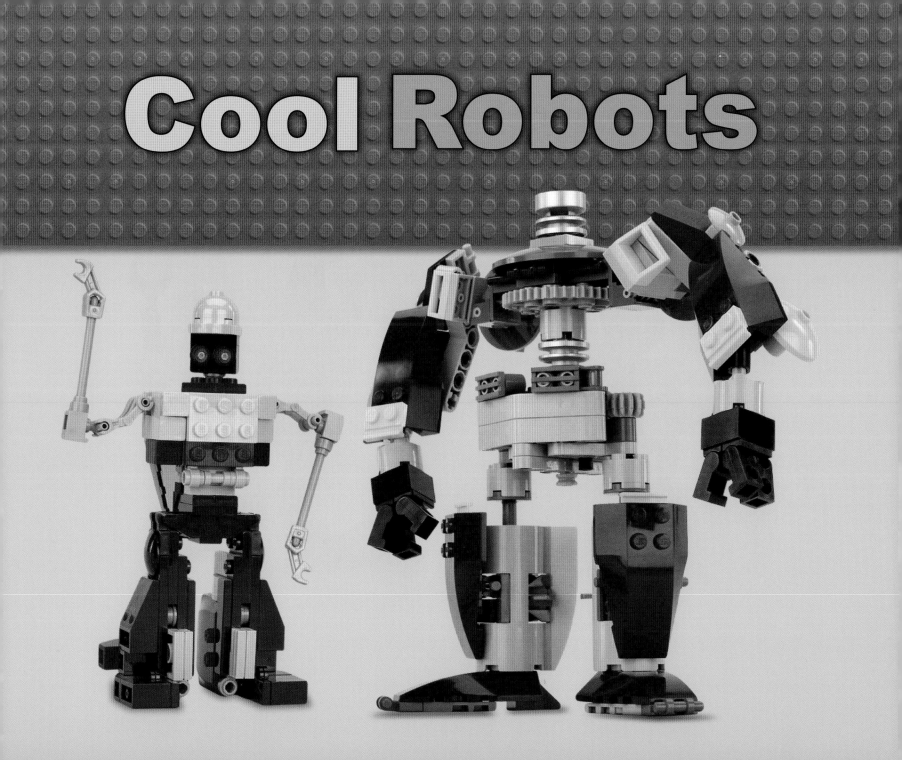

Cool Robots

Let's build some robots!

Welcome to Robotopolis! 46

Family life 48

High-tech robo-furniture 50

On the street 51

Across space, across town 52

Let's build! 54

Special delivery 56

Build a bot 60

Flatten it down 63

Strong bots 64

Pocket-sized crazy bots 66

Build it BIG! 69

Building Robotopolis 70

Build a constructobot 72

A tiny fleet 74

Get creative with tools 75

Take a break at the space station 76

Time to relax at home . . . 78

Welcome to Robotopolis!

This is a busy city full of robots and spaceships.

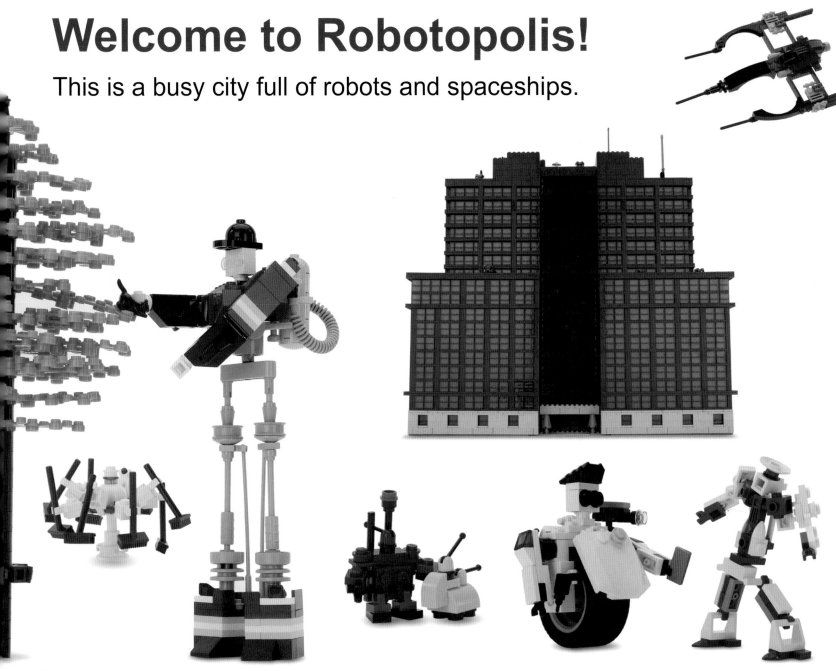

Family life

Even robots like to enjoy an afternoon at home.

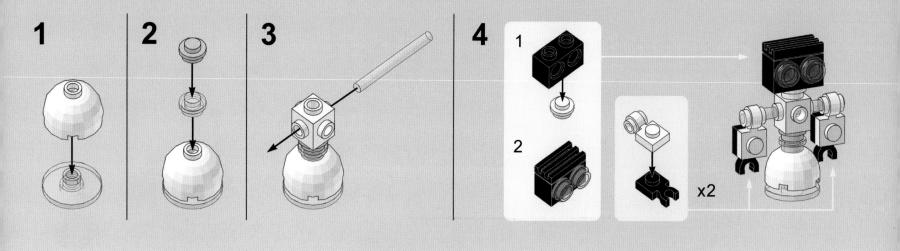

1

2

3

4

Can you build the rest of the family?

High-tech robo-furniture

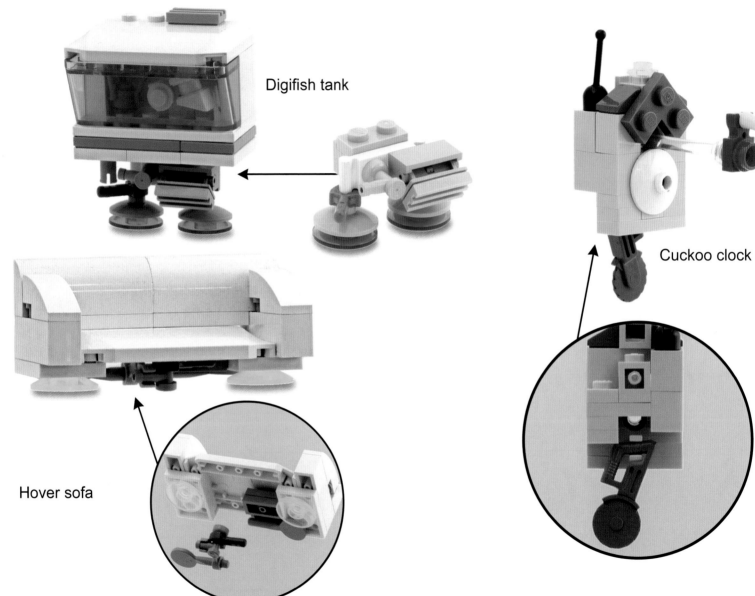

Digifish tank

Cuckoo clock

Hover sofa

On the street

Ticketing and towing
illegally parked hovercars

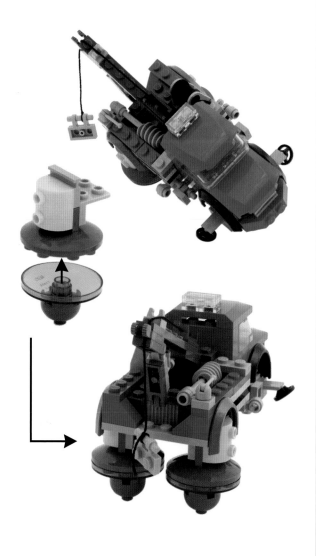

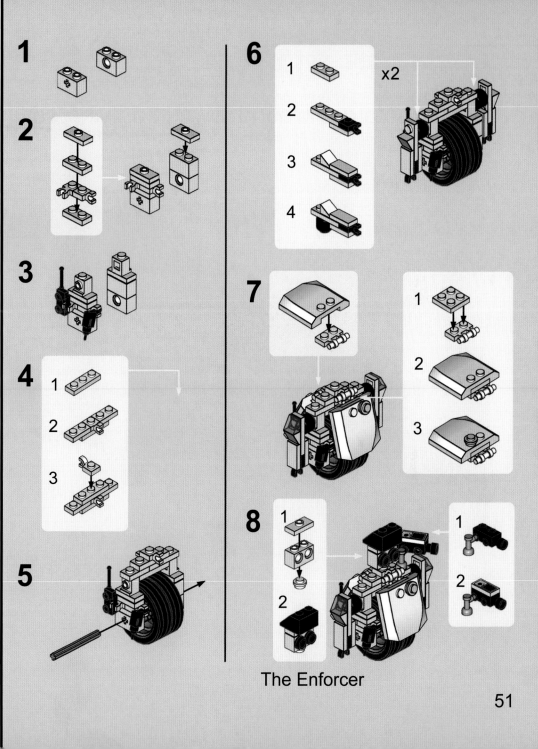

1

2

3

4
1
2
3

5

6
1 x2
2
3
4

7
1
2
3

8
1
2

1
2

The Enforcer

Across space, across town

Most robots get around town in a flying car.

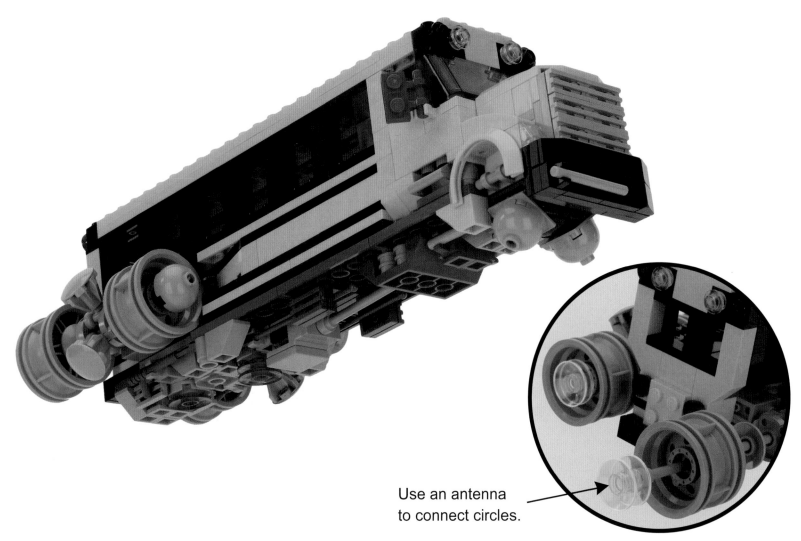

Use an antenna
to connect circles.

Turn any car into a hovercraft by taking off the wheels and adding cool space parts.

What other kinds of flying cars can you make?

Let's build!

You can build your own city of robots and spaceships.

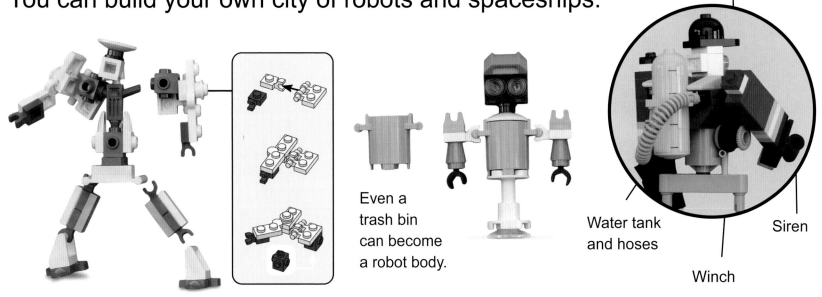

Even a trash bin can become a robot body.

Water tank and hoses

Winch

Emergency lights

Siren

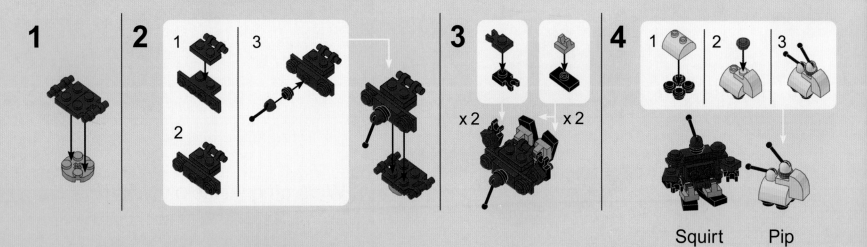

1

2
1
2
3

3
x 2   x 2

4
1   2   3

Squirt   Pip

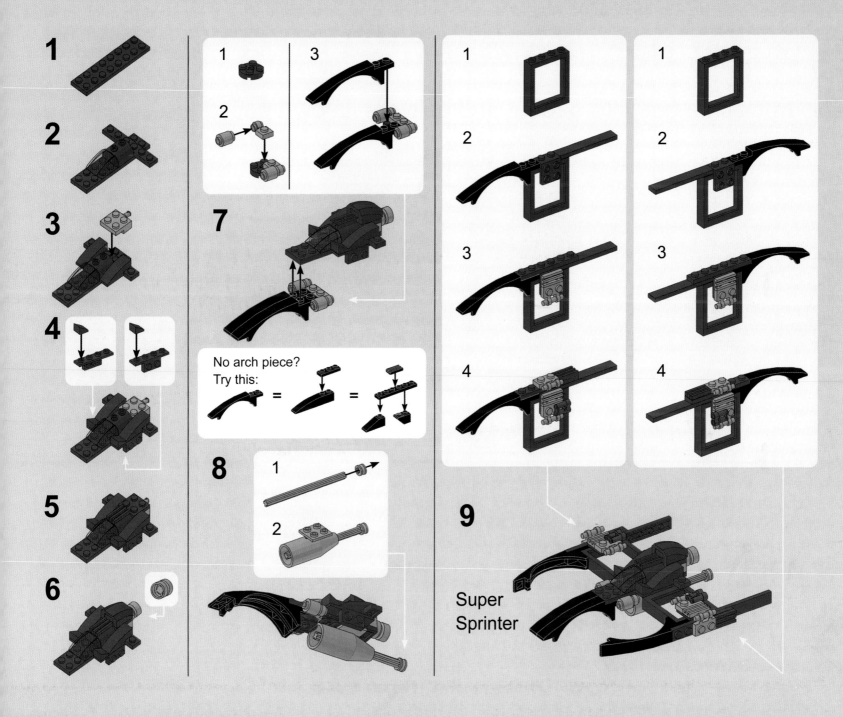

1

2

3

4

5

6

7

8

9

No arch piece?
Try this:

= =

Super
Sprinter

Special delivery

This truck changes into a robot and delivers its own packages.

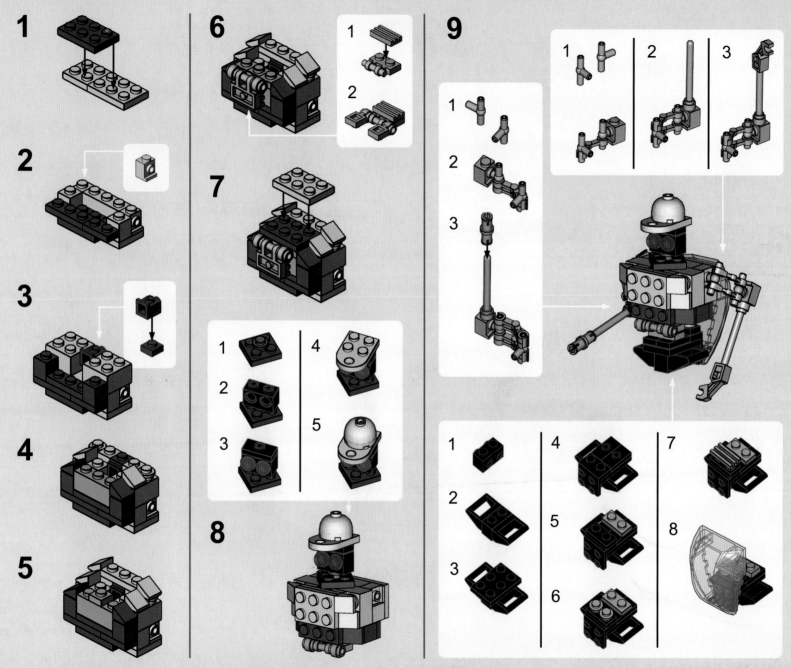

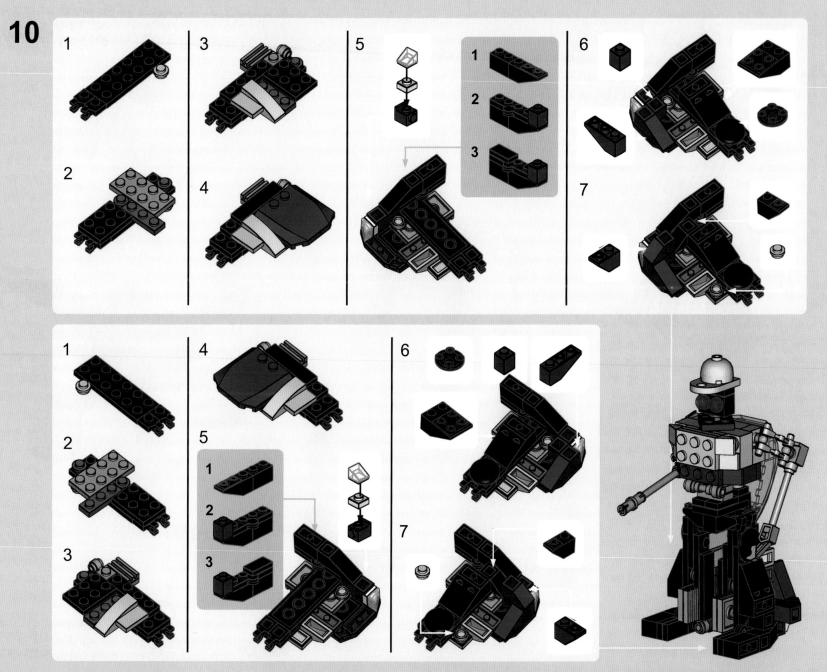

Dynamic Heavy Lifter 59

Build a bot

Mix and match your own pieces.

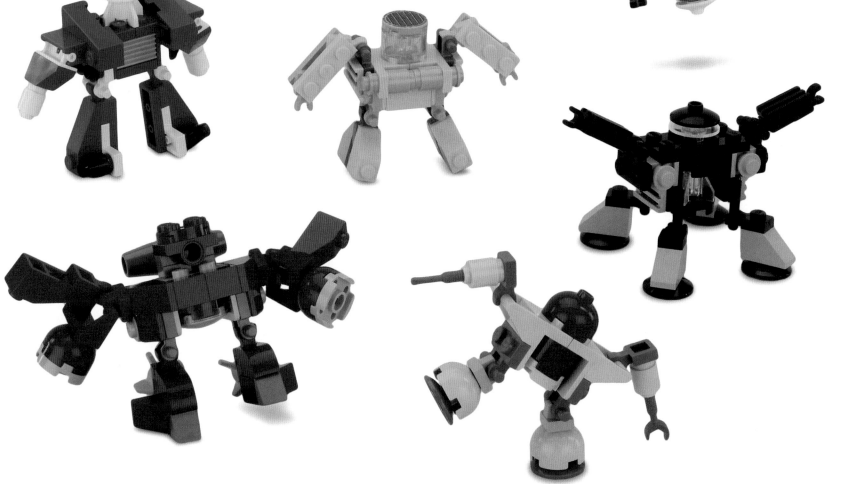

Middle

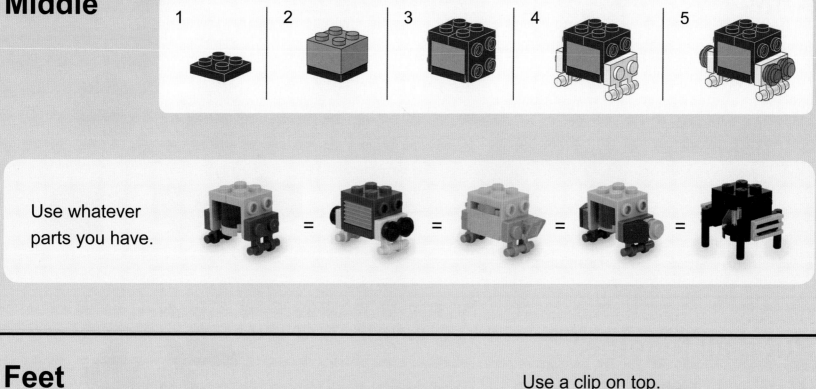

Use whatever parts you have.

Feet

Use a clip on top.

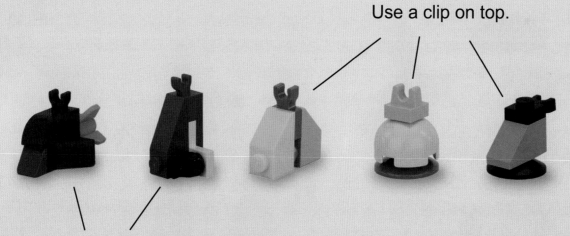

Make them wide to help your robot stand.

Arms

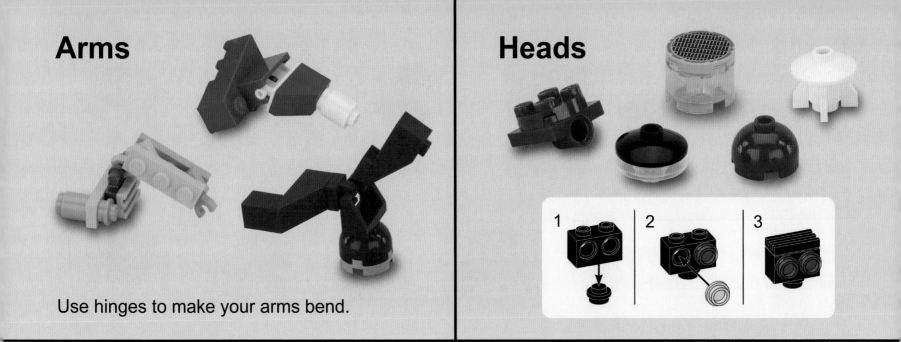

Use hinges to make your arms bend.

Heads

Put it all together

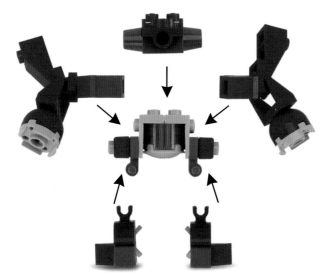

What other robots
can you design?

Flatten it down

Build a mosaic to create a flat picture of a robot.

Strong bots

Big, tough bots help protect Robotopolis
from the forces of evil.

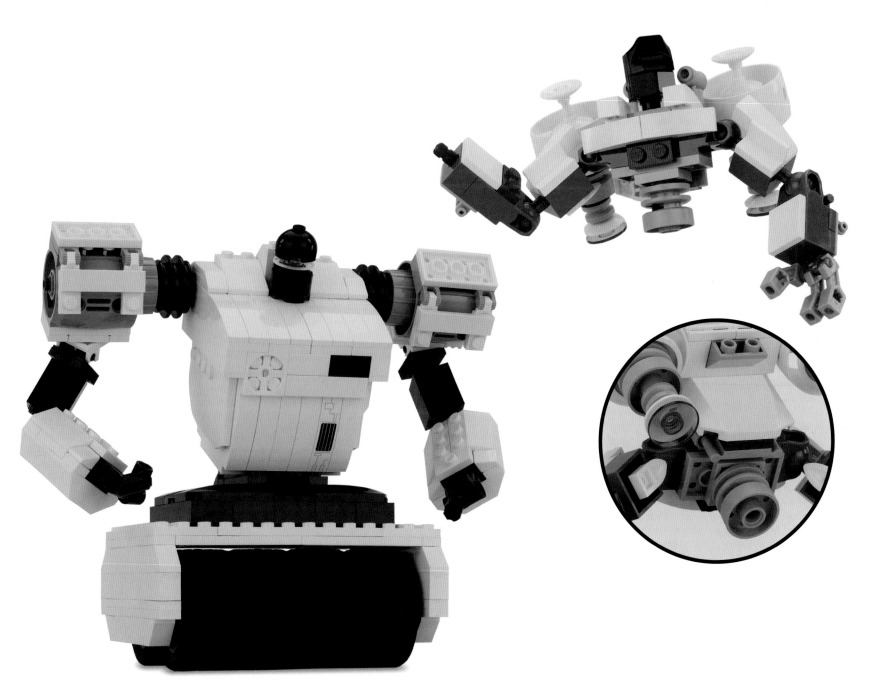

Pocket-sized crazy bots

You only need a few pieces to build a community of robots.

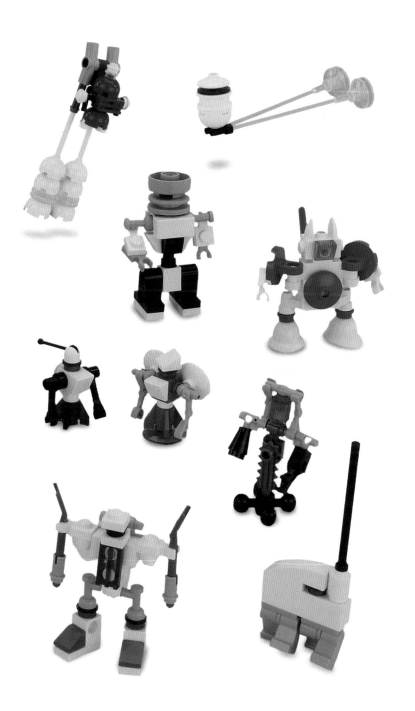

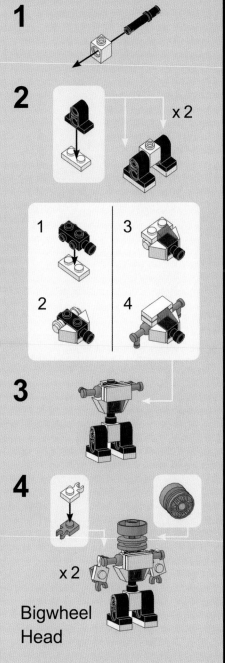

1

2 x 2

1
2
3
4

3

4 x 2

Bigwheel
Head

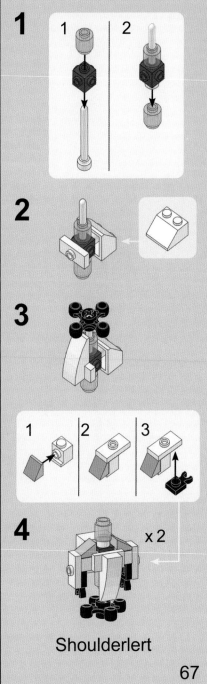

1
1
2

2

3

1
2
3

4 x 2

Shoulderlert

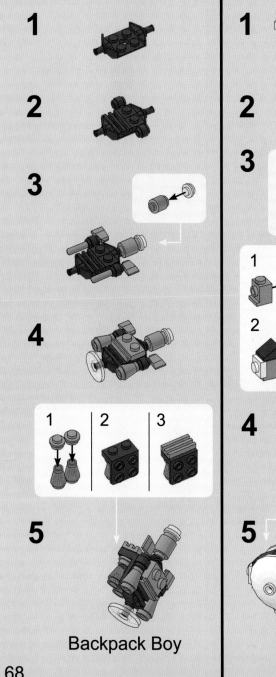

1

2

3

4

5

Backpack Boy

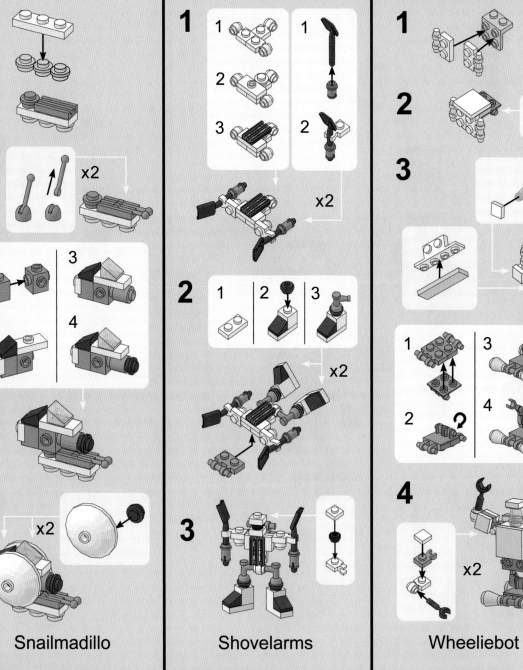

1

2

3

x2

1 **3**

2 **4**

4

5 x2

Snailmadillo

1

1

2

3

1

2

x2

2

1 2 3

x2

3

Shovelarms

1

2

3

1

2

3

4

1

2

4

x2

Wheeliebot

Build it BIG!

Make jumbo-sized pieces, then combine them into a giant robot.

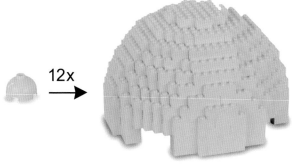

12x →

12x →

Building Robotopolis

These robots are a construction worker and a tough truck, all in one.

Build a constructobot

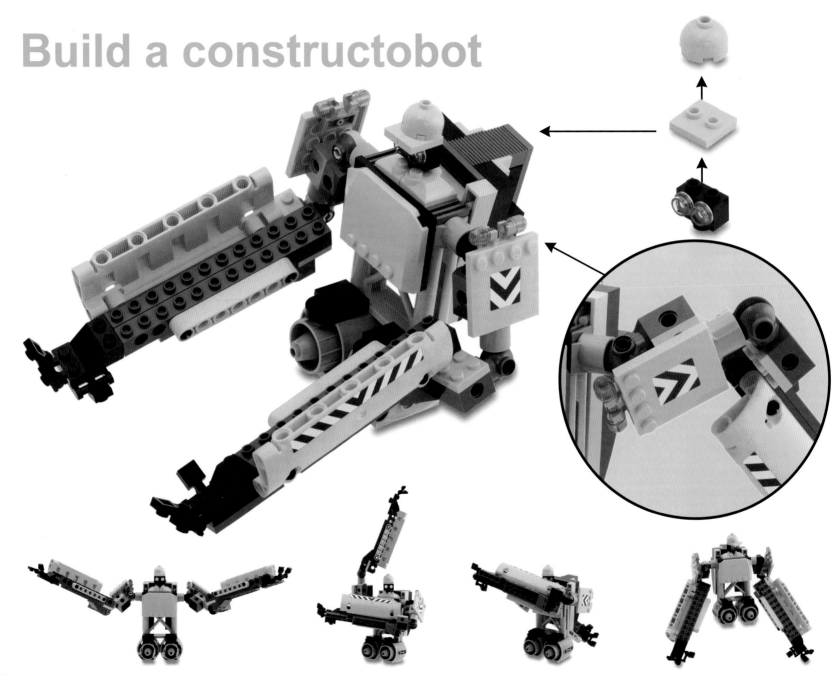

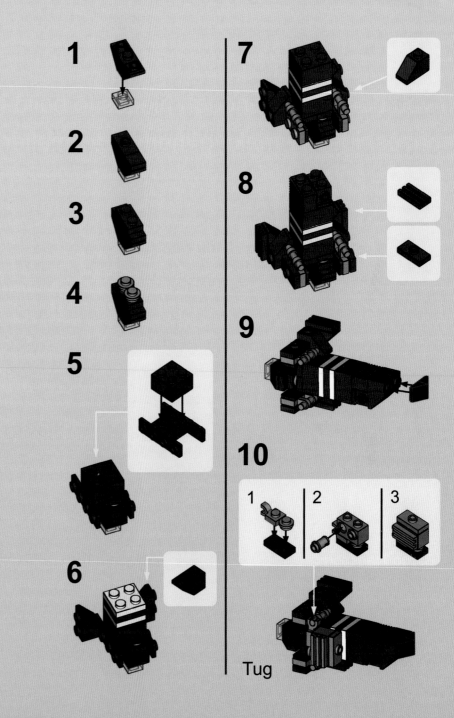

1

2

3

4

5

6

7

8

9

10

1 | 2 | 3

Tug

A tiny fleet

If you don't have enough pieces to build lots of large spaceships, try making them in a smaller size.

Tug

Special Task Force

Cargo Transport

Central Command

High-Speed Scout

Get creative with tools

Accessories make great robot parts.

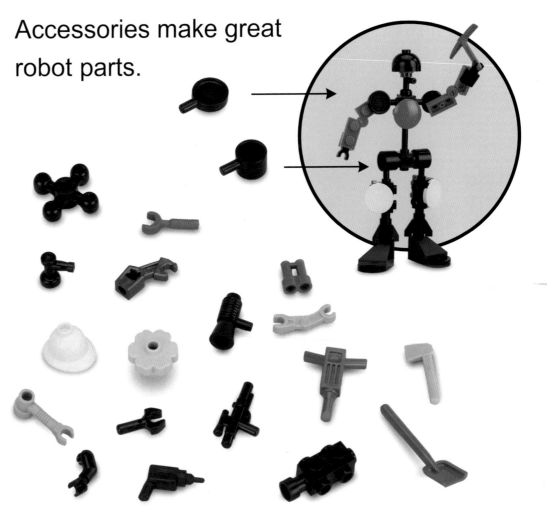

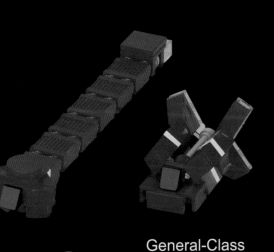

General-Class
Sprinter

Recon Shuttle

Can you find where these parts are used in this book?

Take a break at the space station

Traveling through outer space can take a while.

Why not stop along the way?

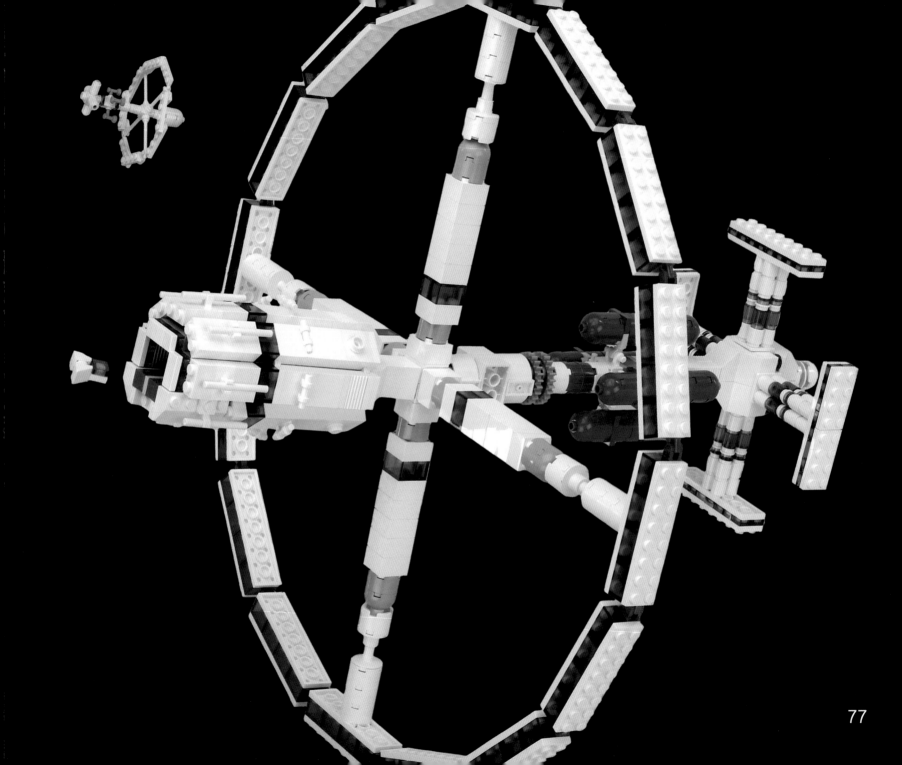

Time to relax at home . . .

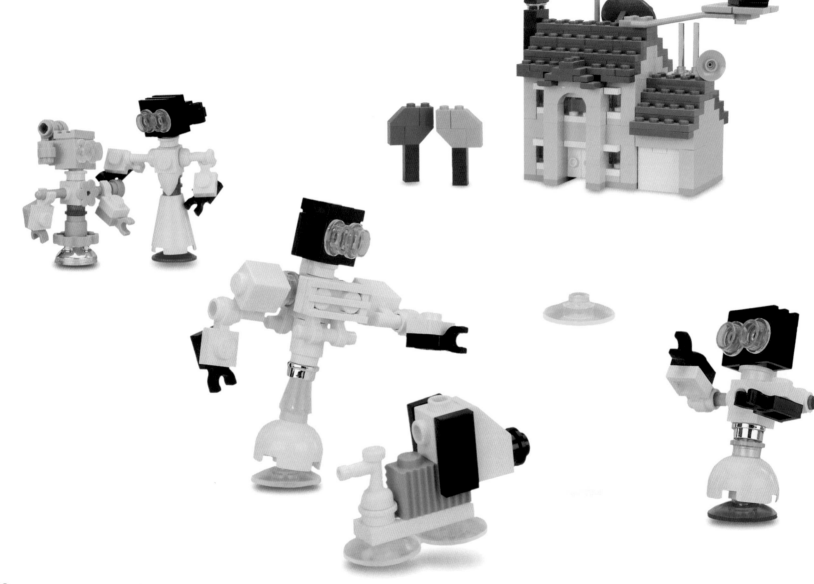

until the next adventure!

Let's build a city!

Town square 84

Things to do 86

Subway station 88

Skyscraper 90

Aerial view 92

Mini metropolis 94

Park details 96

City interiors 97

Build a subway platform 98

City bus 99

Make your own bus 103

Build a streetcar 104

Street furniture 106

Traffic jam 108

All clear! 109

Building styles 110

Modern furniture 112

Office furniture 113

Build some buildings 114

Make a home on Main Street 116

Elevator 118

More than just buildings 120

City plaza 122

The city is a great place to be!

There are lots of things to see and to do . . .

. . . whether you're underground . . .

Subway ↓

Street

Entrance

Station

Ticket machines

Turnstiles

Platform

Pipes and gizmos

. . . or way up high.

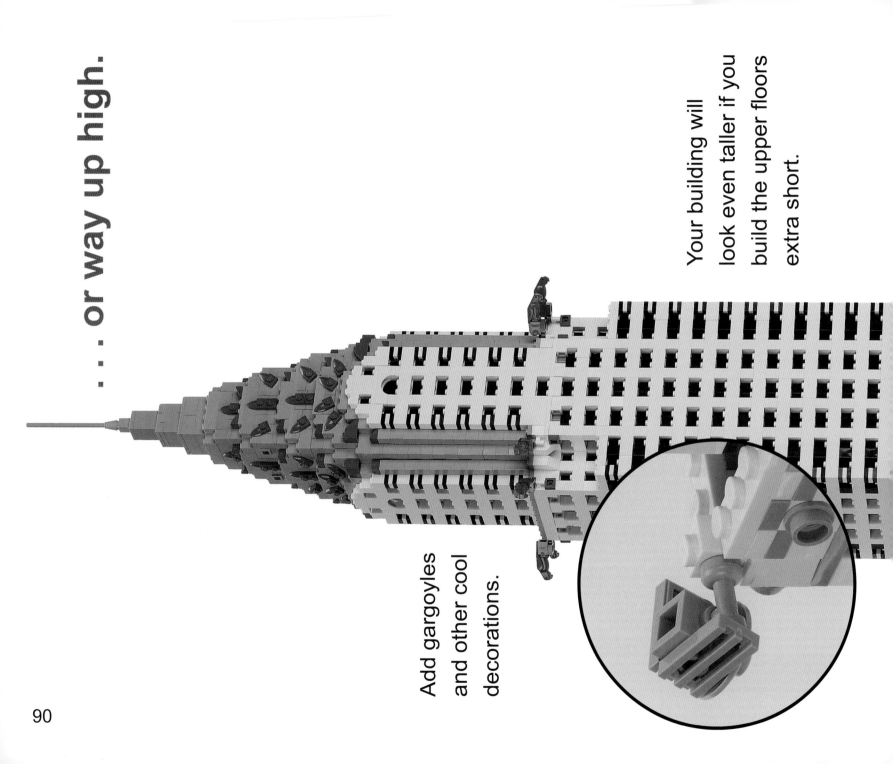

Your building will
look even taller if you
build the upper floors
extra short.

Add gargoyles
and other cool
decorations.

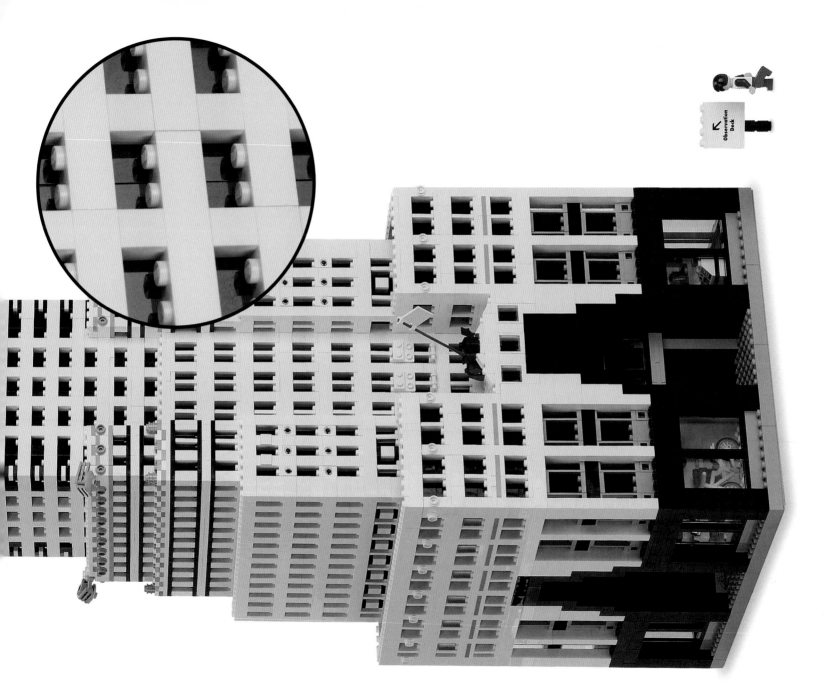

Observation Deck

What a great view of the city!

Make a mini metropolis.

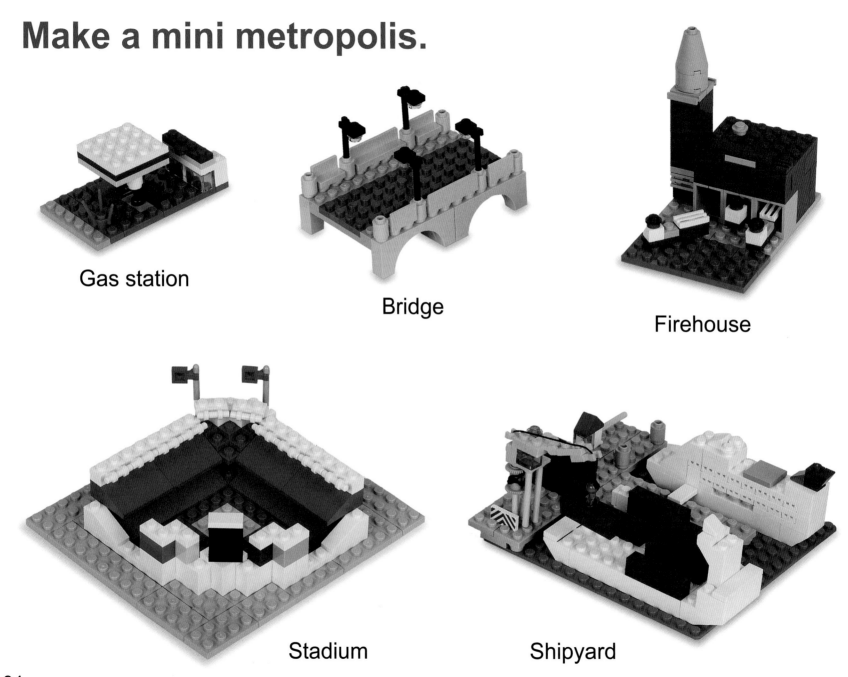

Gas station

Bridge

Firehouse

Stadium

Shipyard

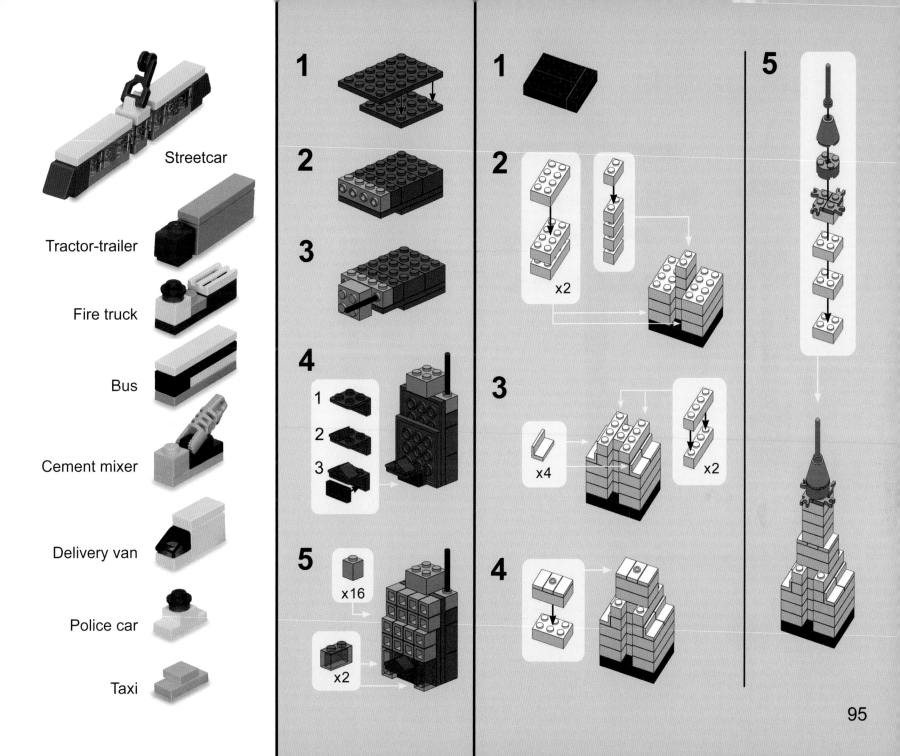

Streetcar

Tractor-trailer

Fire truck

Bus

Cement mixer

Delivery van

Police car

Taxi

1

2

3

4
1
2
3

5
x16
x2

1

2
x2

3
x4
x2

4

5

Park details

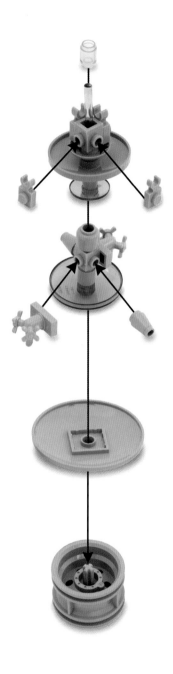

This park lamp is only 4 pieces! Can you build it?

City interiors

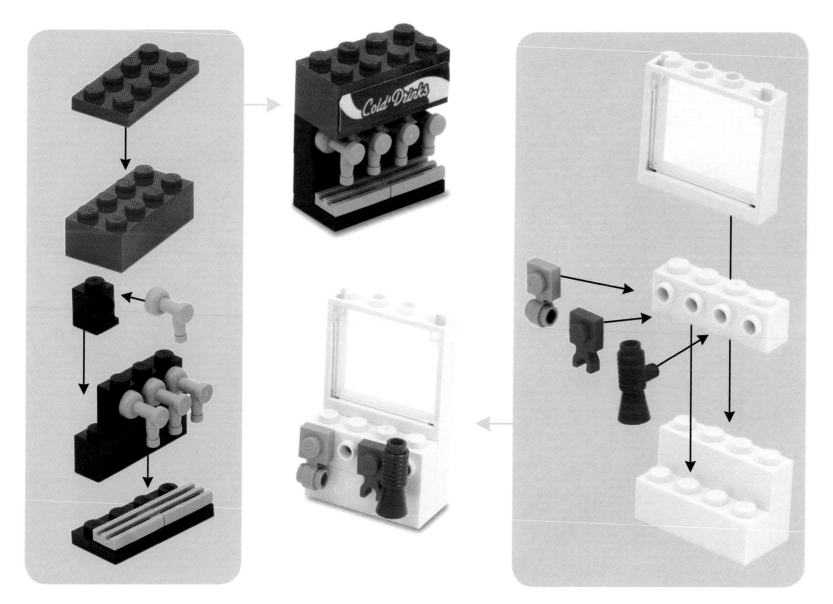

Cold Drinks

Build a subway platform

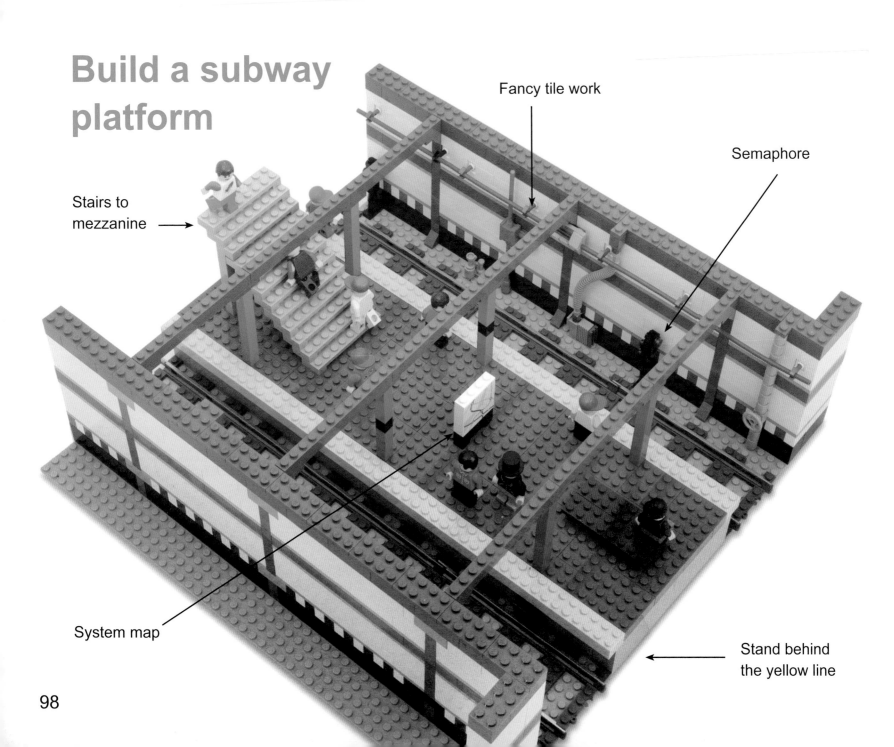

Fancy tile work

Semaphore

Stairs to mezzanine

System map

Stand behind the yellow line

Turnstiles

Ticket machine

Semaphore

1

2

3

City bus

4

5

1

2

6

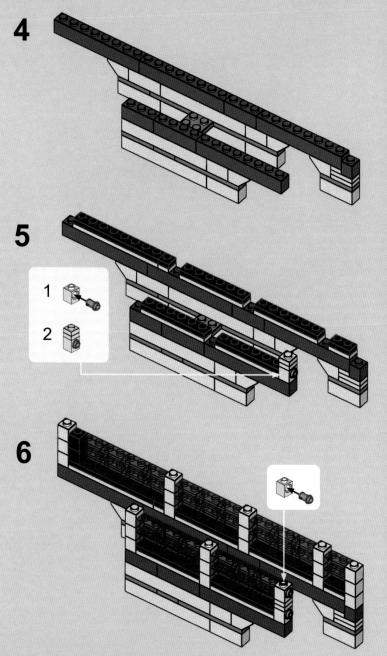

7

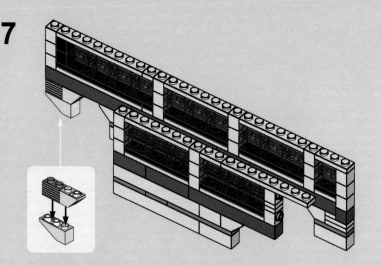

8

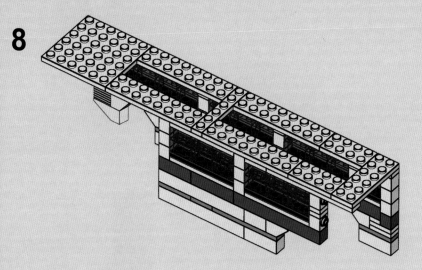

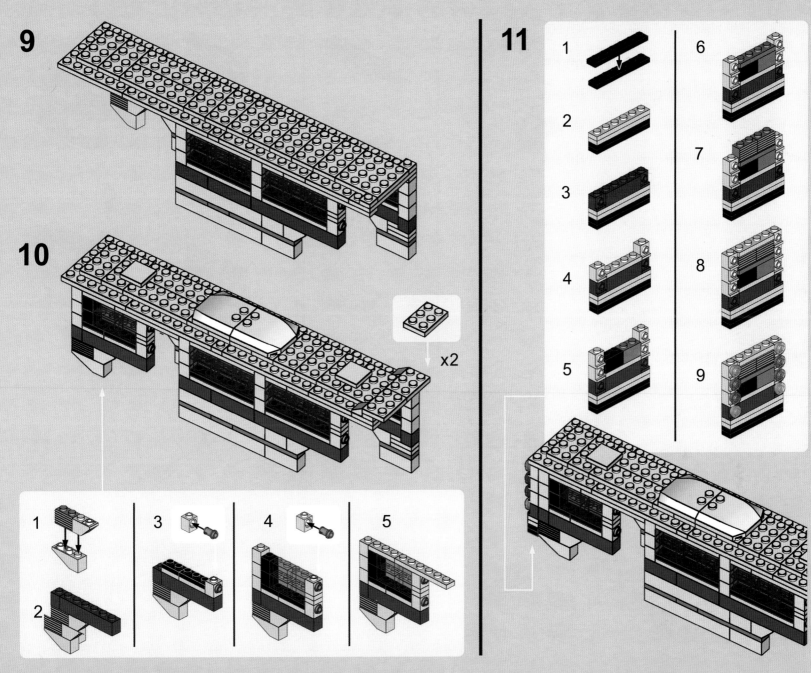

12

1
2
3
4
5

x2

1
2
3

13

1
2
3
4
5
6
7
8
9

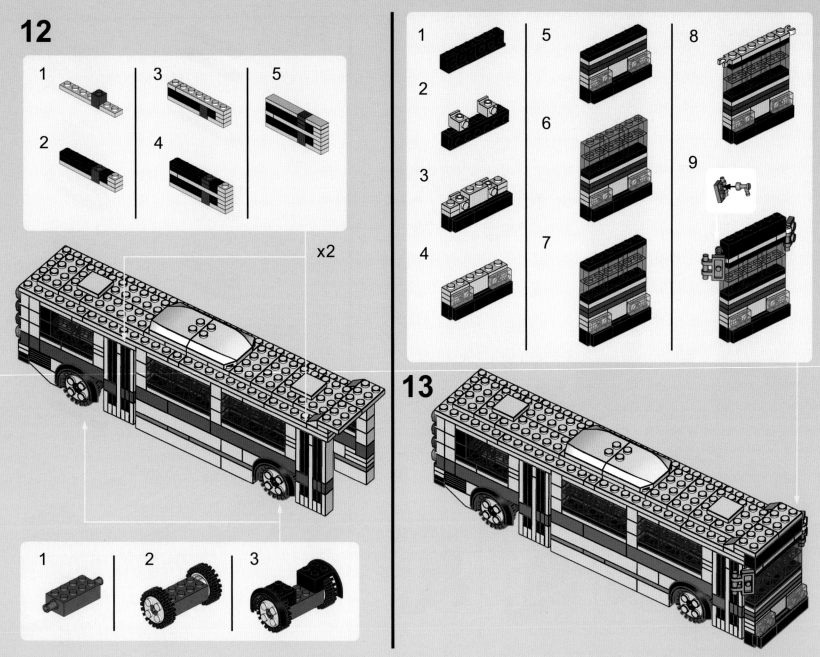

Make your own bus

You can use the same basic design to create many other buses.

Build a streetcar

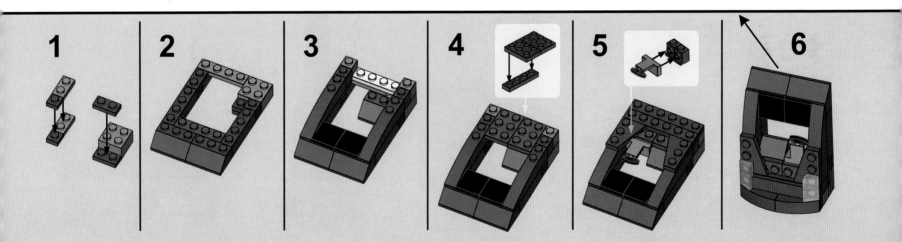

Give your street some furniture.

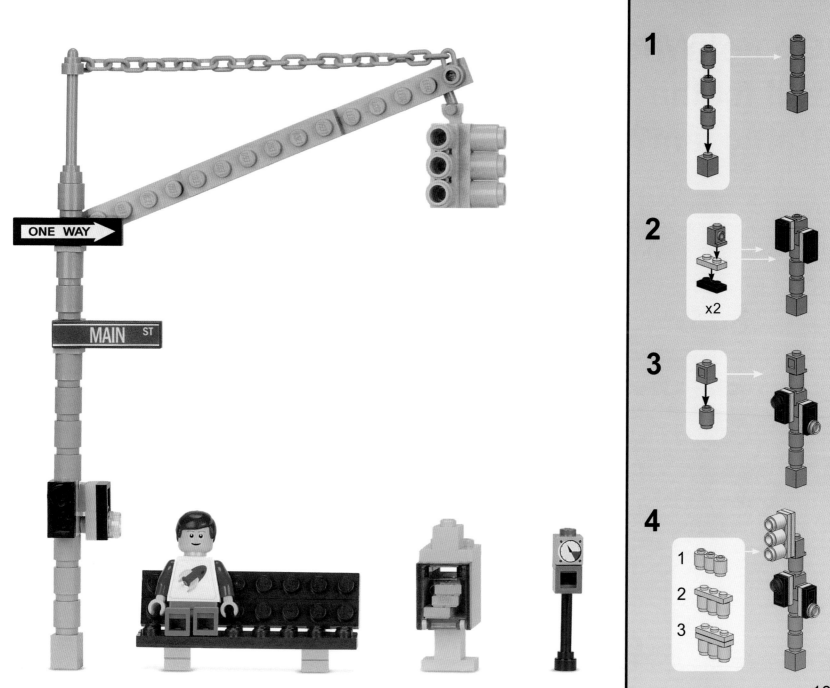

1

2 x2

3

4
1
2
3

Oh no! Who will fix the traffic jam?

All clear!

Different building styles make the city interesting.

New building

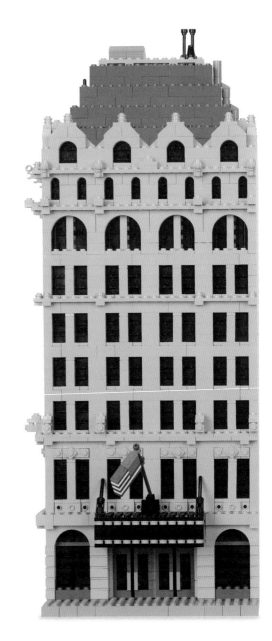

Old building

Big building

Small building

Modern furniture

Give your condo high-rise
some classy furnishings.

Office furniture

Recycle bin

Copier

Executive office

Receptionist's desk

Conference Room

Projecter

Speaker phone

Water cooler

Boardroom

Leather chair

Easel

Reception

Coffeemaker

Laser printer

Build some buildings

Make your own designs with whatever pieces you have.

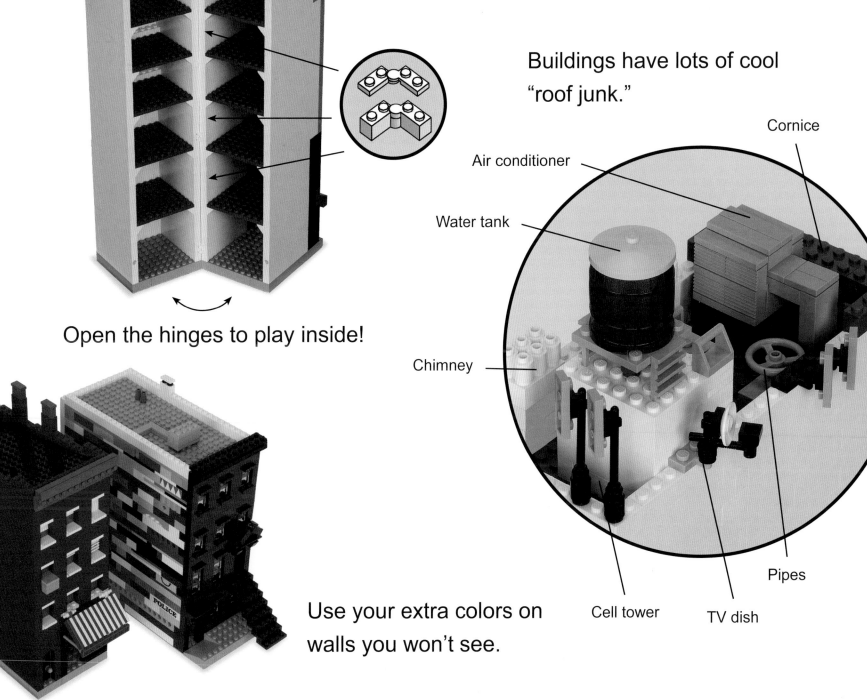

Open the hinges to play inside!

Buildings have lots of cool "roof junk."

Cornice

Air conditioner

Water tank

Chimney

Use your extra colors on walls you won't see.

Cell tower

TV dish

Pipes

Make a home on Main Street

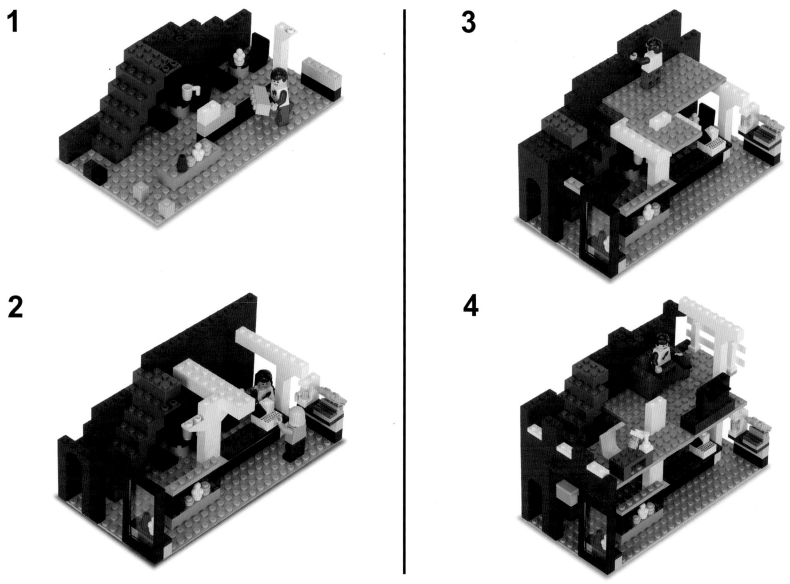

1

2

3

4

5

6

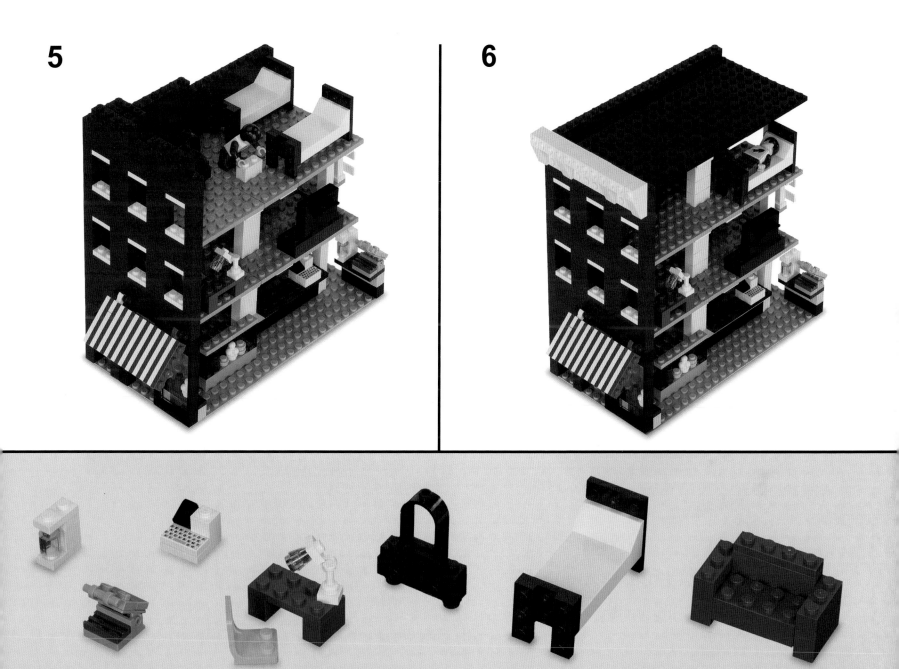

Ride the elevator and visit a home in the sky!

Use a pulley to make your elevator actually work.

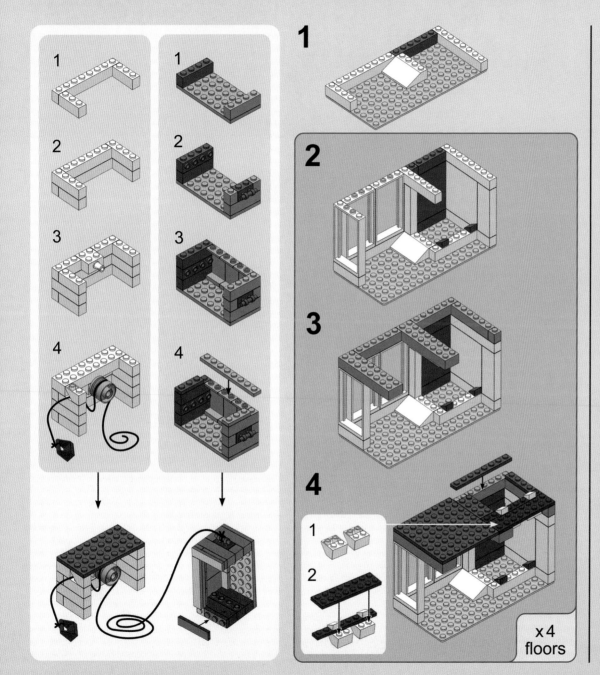

1

2

3

4

1

2

x 4
floors

5

More than just buildings

Things to do and places to go make the city exciting!

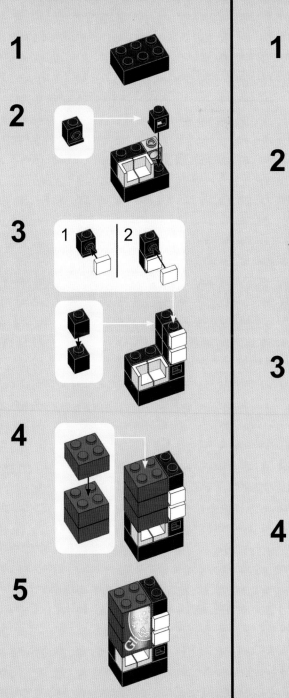

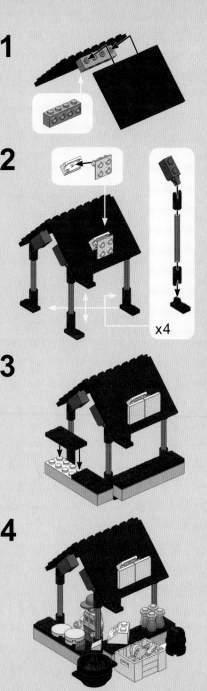

What else can you add to your
city to bring it to life?

Let's Ask Sean

1. What is your earliest memory of playing with LEGO?

I've been building with LEGO all my life. I found a photograph of me stacking together DUPLO pieces when I was two years old, so, at least since then.

2. Do you remember your first LEGO kit? What was it? And what was the coolest model you remember building as a kid?

For my fifth birthday, I really, really wanted the "Exxon Gas Station" (#6375, from 1980). It was a very cool set with a working repair lift, and you could open the cars' hoods, change the tires, and more. The night before my birthday, I begged my parents to let me open one present early. They agreed. I shook my gifts until I heard LEGO, and then tore open the box to find the Exxon Gas Station! I started building it, but before long, it was time to go to bed and I wasn't done. I convinced my parents to let me keep it in my room, so that I could finish building it as soon as I woke up. But, I had a secret plan! As soon as I was tucked in and the lights were out, I slid

Sean at age 11, and his city

the box onto my bed and started building by the moonlight. It was too dark to read the instructions, so I tiptoed over and turned on the light. Soon, my parents heard LEGO noises. I ran across the room, switched off the light, and jumped under the covers just in time to see my dad open the door, look around, and close the door again. Phew! Convinced I could keep it up, I turned the light back on and kept building. But my parents heard the LEGO noises again. As they were coming back to check on me, I again ran across the room to turn out the light. Suddenly, as my hand was outstretched and about to flick off the switch, my dad opened the door! "Give me the LEGO set," he said. Defeated, I had to wait until the next morning to finish building my gas station. I still have some of the pieces from that set on display in my million-piece LEGO studio.

3. What did you study in college and how did that lead to your becoming a LEGO artist?

I studied a lot of different things, but mostly computer science, visual art, and philosophy. (A little history and music, too.) When I was growing up in the 1980s, few people had computers. But my parents owned a small computer and taught me how to write computer programs. I really loved the computer, which is why I majored in computer science in college. Knowing computer technology is very useful and has helped me run the business part of selling my work. And taking art classes in college helped me learn more about photography, creating graphics for the Web, and drawing techniques. I draw all the time when planning my LEGO sculptures.

4. Other than LEGO building, what else did you do as a child that inspired you to become a LEGO artist?

I used to draw ALL the time. I would invent my own imaginary robots, draw cartoons of my friends and teachers, and lots more; everyone knew me as the cartoon guy. I loved cities and buildings, and learned about mechanical drawing and architecture when I was in high school. Now, in creating my LEGO artwork, I draw all the time to plan what my sculptures will look like, to illustrate ideas, and to share my designs with my assistants. I still love to draw and do it nearly every day.

5. What do you like most about building with LEGO?

What's not to like? I get to play with toys all day! I especially enjoy creating sculptures that make others smile. It's great to know I can do what I love, have fun, and make people happy.

VROOOOOM!

6. You have created many impressive installations for major corporations, as well as cities, all over the world. Can you highlight some of your favorite projects?

I created an Empire State Building model at the top of the Empire State Building. I built a whole series of super-sized plants, insects, and animals that are touring botanical gardens around the United States. I made a 6-foot-tall model of the Nintendo DSI that stood in the windows of their store at Rockefeller Center, facing the streets of Manhattan. I designed a giant bedroom loft that's permanently part of someone's home. I've made a few Google logos that are hanging in their offices around the world. Once, the car manufacturer Mazda asked me to create a model of the Mazda3 for every auto dealership across Mexico. (There was a contest involved where if you guessed how many LEGO pieces were used to make the model, you could win a real car!) I've shipped sculptures, portraits, busts, logos, lamps, and cake toppers to people all around the United States, as well as to Japan, China, Australia, Brazil, Argentina, Mexico, Canada, Italy, Germany, England, Belgium, Switzerland, and even Mongolia.

7. What is the challenge of building in large scale? How do you create a blueprint to follow working at that scale?

Building BIG can be a challenge, often because the sculptures get too heavy to lift, and too big to fit through a door. Sometimes, I have to make the sculpture in large pieces so I can take them apart and then reassemble them (harder

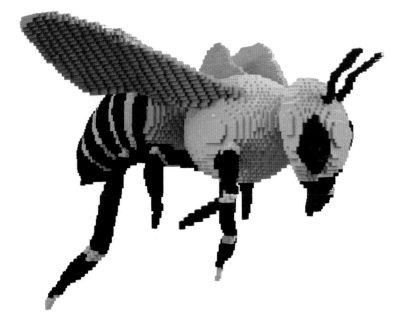

than it sounds). The models usually require custom, foam-lined wooden crates just to ship them around the world (or just across town). When building big sculptures, I need to plan ahead. Often, I'll make a miniature test model, or prototype a small section in its actual size, and make lots of drawings on graph paper.

8. What model/project took the most time for you to create and why?

The biggest project I've created is a traveling show called "Nature Connects," which features over 25 larger-than-life sculptures of plants, animals, and insects. There's an 8-foot-tall hummingbird feeding off a flower, a 5-foot-wide butterfly, a 7-foot-tall rose, a giant bee hanging from the ceiling—the show was built with nearly half a million LEGO pieces! It took my team and me about 5,000 hours to build it. That's two and a half years of full-time work! The show is touring botanical gardens around the United States from 2013 to 2016 (and possibly longer).

9. What is your favorite brick piece? What about your favorite brick color?

The headlight brick is my favorite LEGO piece. You can use it to attach small details onto your model sideways (like the headlight of a car). You can also turn it around backward to get a little square-hole shape (great for windows on micro buildings or tiny trains). And if you lay the piece on its back, you get a perfectly aligned stud facing out of your model that you can use to do all kinds of tricks that make your models look like they're stuck together by magic. I don't know if I have a favorite color, but I've found that the sculptures I like best are the ones that combine red, white, and blue together

with a little pop of grey or black for accent details. There's something classic-looking about it.

10. How many hours and bricks did it take to build the life-size polar bear that is in your traveling endangered animals show?

The polar bear weighs nearly 400 pounds and took 1,100 hours (and 40 gallons of coffee) to build. That means if you started building after breakfast on your first day of summer

break and worked every day, all day, breakfast to dinner (no TV!), you wouldn't be done until New Year's Eve! I built it with a bunch of helpers in about a month. The polar bear is built onto an ice floe, set up as if he was stranded on a

melting polar ice cap. It was important to me that the polar bear not only look realistic, but also a little perplexed, sad, and concerned, given that he is endangered. I spent two days on just the eyes to get the expression right.

11. Is there a subject that you'd love to tackle—for instance, a LEGO replica of the Taj Mahal or Mount Rushmore? What's on your short list to build?

There are so many things I'd love to build if I had enough time. New York's Grand Central Station, a cherry blossom tree in full bloom, life-size furniture, giant dim sum servings, a life-size bus or streetcar, Ming Dynasty architecture, a portrait of my family. And house keys made of mouse cheese.

12. What advice would you give to young LEGO builders who hope to follow in your footsteps some day?

I've learned most of my building techniques simply by building, building, and building. Every new project still teaches you a better (or worse) way of doing something, and over time, you can learn which techniques to use in which situations. Don't be afraid of making mistakes; you learn more from mistakes than from your successes. LEGO pieces can be put right back together again. With a good idea and a little patience, you can create anything.

About Sean

Sean Kenney likes to prove you can build anything with LEGO bricks. He makes LEGO sculptures and models at his studio in New York City.

Sean picked up his first LEGO bricks as a child, and his passion for LEGO grew through the years as he grew. He is now recognized as one of the premier LEGO brick builders in the world.

Visit Sean at seankenney.com to:

- Share your cool creations with kids around the world
- Order some extra LEGO pieces
- Find out if Sean is coming to your neighborhood and lots more!